TENNESSEE FOOTBALL

THE PEYTON MANNING YEARS

ACKNOWLEDGMENTS

It is with great pride that we present you with this special book—*Tennessee Football: The Peyton Manning Years.* Our goal was to produce the best book ever written about Tennessee Football and one of the most outstanding young men ever to play the game for the Vols. Or anybody else. It's all here from start to finish.

This book is a result of a lot of hard work of many dedicated people to whom we are extremely grateful. First of all we would like to thank all the people at the University including Doug Dickey, Head Football Coach Phillip Fulmer, Bud Ford, Jim Bletner, and everyone else involved with UT football.

This book was written by Tom Mattingly, UT's Director of Special Publications, who we believe knows as much about Tennessee football as anyone. Tom worked hand in hand with photographers Don Carringer, Steve Carringer, and Randy Russell, collectively known as Football Time in Tennessee, Brian Spurlock, Donnell Field and Michael Herbert to bring you this wonderful story.

We would also like to extend a special thanks to all the people at The Collegiate Licensing Co. including Mr. Bill Battle and Mr. Cory Moss, for allowing us to undertake this project.

Finally, we would like to thank Peyton Manning, his father, Archie, and his mother, Olivia. They were most helpful and gracious allowing us in their home and access to their personal family albums and scrapbooks to bring you never-before-published behind-the-scenes photos of Peyton and the rest of the family.

Please enjoy.

 Tennessee Football: The Peyton Manning Years is officially licensed by the University of Tennessee and the Collegiate Licensing Co.

PHOTO CREDITS

Michael C. Hebert—7, 14 (top), 19 (top), 48, 49, 52 (bottom), 80 (bottom), 120, 121, 123 (bottom), 125, 140, 143

Football Time in Tennessee—8, 9, 10, 12 (bottom), 13 (x2), 15, 16, 18, 19 (bottom), 22, 23 (x2), 24, 25 (x2), 26, 27, 28, 29, 30, 32, 33, 34, 35, 37, 38, 39, 40, 43, 44, 47, 50 (x2), 51 (x2), 52 (top), 54, 55, 56, 58, 59, 60, 61, 62, 63, 64 (x2), 65, 68, 69 (x2), 70, 71, 72 (bottom), 73, 74, 75 (x2), 76, 78, 79, 80 (top), 81, 82 (x2), 83, 84, 85, 105, 106, 108, 109 (x2), 110, 111, 112 (x2), 113, 124, 126, 127, 128 (x2), 129, 130, 131, 132 (x2), 133, 134 (x2), 135, 136, 137, 139

Brian Spurlock—12 (top), 14 (bottom), 46, 57, 67, 72 (top), 107 (x2), 117 (x2), 118, 119, 122, 123 (top), 144, 147, 148, 155, 156, 151, 159

Barry Lawrence—152

Donnell Field—36

Manning Family Photos—86–103

Staff: *Publisher/President:* Ivan Mothershead; *Associate Publisher/Executive Vice President:* Charlie Keiger; *Vice President:* Rick Peters; *Controller:* Lewis Patton; *Advertising Manager:* Mark Cantey; *Advertising Executive:* Paul Kaperonis; *Managing Editor:* Ward Woodbury; *Art Director:* Brett Shippy; *Senior Designers:* Mike McBride and Paul Bond; *Manager of Information Systems:* Henry Boardman; *Administrative Staff:* Mary Cartee, Carla Greene; *Electronic Pre-Press and Design,* Andrew Barnes/Rainbow Graphics, LLC, Kingsport, Tennessee.

ISBN 0-943860-13-X

CONTENTS

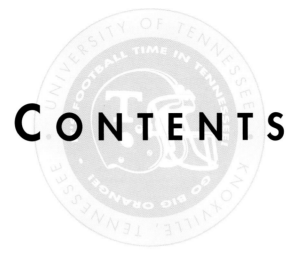

AUTHOR'S PREFACE

This book came about as part of a chance meeting with Charlie Keiger in the halls of Stokely Athletic Center in Knoxville this past winter. I relished the thought of assembling a manuscript about Peyton Manning, arguably the most popular athlete in Tennessee history, even considering that it is risky business, as noted sportscaster and Tennessee alumnus (Class of 1941) Lindsey Nelson once observed, to compare athletes across the generations.

It is a daunting task to assemble a word picture of a young man with so many facets to his personality. After all, Peyton distinguished himself as a student and an athlete as well as a role model. He even does a pretty fair impersonation of former Ole Miss broadcaster Stan Torgerson, calling a long-ago Rebel game with Archie Manning under center. During his time at Tennessee, Peyton did it all and did it with great aplomb. There's really no one quite like him. No one got it done on the field and in the classroom like Peyton Williams Manning. You almost run out of adjectives trying to describe him.

As editor of *Volunteers Magazine*, I was able to see the Peyton Manning phenomenon first-hand, from the time he arrived on campus, through those first tentative steps on the verdant turf of the Rose Bowl in the 1994 season opener, through his taking the Vols to a 7–1 record as a starter that season, to records of 11–1, 10–2 and 11–2 the next three years. (The 32–5 run over that time is the most victories in a three-year span in Vol history.)

There was that magic moment when he announced he was coming back for his senior season and an equally magic moment when the Vols brought home the SEC Championship in December of last year in Atlanta. There were, when you think about it, enough magic moments for even the most hardened Vol fans. There was a bump or two along the way, but the journey was an exciting one.

All of us marveled as Peyton grew into his role as the Vol signal-caller, taking his place with the legends of the past. He showed a competitive zeal and a will to prepare to win that all of us came to admire. Even when things might have not gone his way, he was always ready to prepare to compete again another day.

With the heady wine of success and the bitter fruit of defeat, he was always the same. I'll remember his disappointment after the 1997 Florida game and I'll remember more the way Peyton, Leonard Little, and the rest of the Vols recoiled to win the next nine games, annex the SEC crown and win a trip to the Orange Bowl.

I watched him in press rooms under stadia across the country and watched his amazing performance on "The David Letterman Show" in New York last December. Nothing seemed to faze him at all that night, except the possibility of meeting country music's newest singing sensation, Shania Twain. He handled that little chore quite well, too.

I watched him at the Hall of Fame Awards Banquet the next day and evening and marveled as he was the

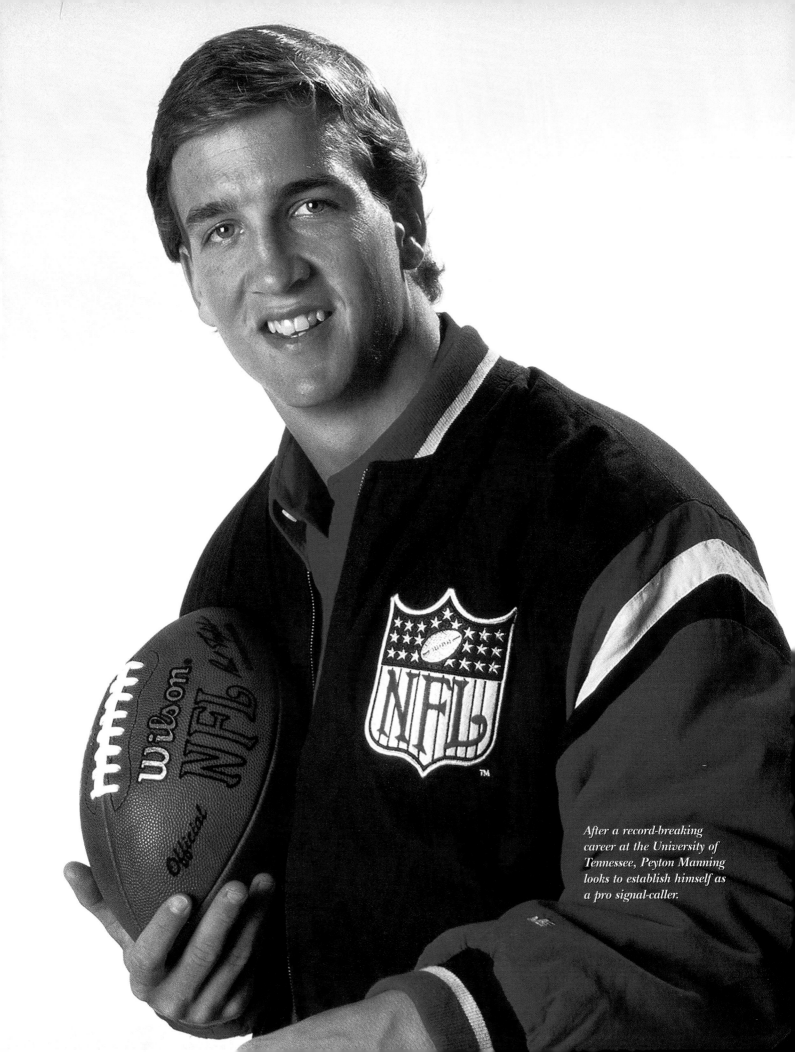

After a record-breaking career at the University of Tennessee, Peyton Manning looks to establish himself as a pro signal-caller.

center of attention from his fellow athletes and many of the adults at a noon luncheon at which he was named Division 1-A Scholar Athlete of the Year. As you will soon see, he was equally impressive when he received the Burger King Vincent dePaul Draddy National Scholar–Athlete of the Year Award that night.

In the narrative, I try to recount the grace with which he handled another bump in the road, the night of the Heisman Awards presentation on ESPN. He didn't win, but, in many ways, in the larger picture, he really did.

When he won the James E. Sullivan Award as the nation's top amateur athlete, he surprised nearly everybody with an eloquent discourse on who James E. Sullivan was and why he was honored to receive the award.

There were those who professed surprise when Peyton made the call to return for another season at UT that day in early March 1997, but, if you knew him, you shouldn't have been shocked at all. People really can't step outside of their character, to readily abandon what makes them unique. (It also helps not being shocked when you can sneak a peek at the speech just before he delivers it.)

Those are a few of the reasons I say "thanks" to Peyton Manning for providing the inspiration for the narrative which follows, but also to Archie and Olivia, Cooper and Eli, as well as a host of teachers, coaches, and other people who helped influence Peyton along the way. But there are others as well.

I thought back to October 5, 1957, and the first Tennessee game I ever saw, the 14–9 win over Mississippi State that was not in the win column until Bobby Gordon took a punt back 55 yards to the north end for the game-winning score. There have been a lot of games since then and the excitement of watching young men in Orange shirts has not diminished in the least.

I thought about attending games with my dad, the late Rev. T. J. Mattingly of Knoxville, from 1957 until he died in 1966. We'd park at Lee Burns' house on Clinch Avenue, walk down 15th Street, and down Stadium Drive to Section V (Row 11) on the west side. I thought about my mother, Dorothy Mattingly, who tolerated the excessive "fandom" around our house, yet always wondered what the fuss was all about. My second oldest sister, Betsy, graduated from the University of Alabama (Class of 1963 and I've since forgiven her) and my

▲ *Manning exhorts his teammates.*

▲ *Head coach Phillip Fulmer makes a point on the Vol sidelines.*

but they still enjoy the tradition and pageantry of Tennessee football.

I thought about Col. Tom Elam, the long-time trustee from Union City, and Knoxvillian Bronson Potter, the latter of whose Vol lineage traces to Bill May and games in 1914 on Wait Field. Both men saw Gene McEver and Peyton Manning play in an Orange shirt on gridirons across the south. That encompasses a lot of history and they were there for all of it. Tom Elam is gone now (he died March 9, 1998), but Bronson Potter lives on in West Knoxville. They are part of a host of memories of my years with Vol football.

oldest sister, Gayle, showed my family and me around Dallas when we were there for the 1990 Cotton Bowl.

I thought about how my own family, wife Susan and children Sam and Alice Compton, has endured many long nights after games, what with the preparation of the weekly *Volunteers Magazine* that has occasionally lasted many times into the early hours of Monday morning. They've probably learned more than they wanted to know about the inner workings of Tennessee athletics,

▲ *Peyton looks down the field for a receiver.*

▲ *Tennessee fans are some of the best in the country, following the Vols wherever they play.*

I wouldn't be here at all if Haywood Harris and Bud Ford hadn't taken a chance on a former Mayoral speechwriter back in 1987. Never mind that I had never edited a magazine before. It's been quite a run since that time.

It's also been quite a run since that day in early March when Charlie and I cut our deal. The journey to this final product has been worth it. I hope you agree.

T.J.M.
May 1998

PREFACE

PREFACE: A PERSPECTIVE ON PEYTON MANNING

In a career replete with great moments, this was perhaps Peyton Manning's finest hour. Bar none. The conventional wisdom was that the young Manning, who had just completed his junior year at UT and was 19 days removed from his 21st birthday, was not returning for his senior season at UT and would thus make himself available for the 1997 NFL draft. The media in attendance were reporting almost unanimously that Manning was leaving and that the media conference was a mere formality. After all, who could turn down the big bucks and the lavish lifestyle offered by the NFL?

66 *I'm not going to try to make this a dramatic ordeal, but there are a few comments I'd like to make. The one thing that's been running through my mind over and over the past couple of months has been the 'hurry up and know, Peyton, hurry up and know.' That's what I've been telling myself. Yesterday morning, I woke up with a huge sense of relief because I finally knew what I was going to do. I've had an incredible experience at the University of Tennessee with all the people I've met, learned from, and become friends with here. College football has been great to me. So have the people, the coaches, and the players I've played with the last three years. I also would have a great experience in pro football. As difficult as it has been, I knew I couldn't make a bad decision. I knew whatever decision I made, it had to be my own decision and nobody else's. I want to thank the people closest to me, especially my mother and father for allowing that to happen. I thoroughly researched the situation and gathered a great deal of information. I've asked dozens of people what they thought and I've prayed a lot about it also. I knew I wanted to be 100 percent sure in my decision. Somebody asked me this morning what was the one thing that helped sway my opinion and helped me decide. There wasn't one thing. Just like when I signed here, it was just sort of a feeling. I made up my mind and don't ever expect to look back. I am going to stay at the University of Tennessee.* 99

—*Peyton Manning*
March 5, 1997

11

Everyone in attendance should have known better. When Manning said "I'm going to stay at the University of Tennessee," the assembled multitudes in the Ray Mears Room at the Thompson–Boling Arena in Knoxville broke into applause and prospects for the 1997 season brightened immediately. The media were stunned. It was a magic moment. It was a media conference with a surprise twist, a turn that no one had expected.

▲ *Peyton heads toward Neyland Stadium on the "Vol Walk" as Vol fans line the sides of "Peyton Manning Pass."*

▲ *Manning takes a last look at the bench before heading to the huddle.*

"When Manning said thanks, but not now, to the NFL," UT's Haywood Harris wrote as part of a preface to the 1997 Tennessee Football Guide, "his actions gave testimony to his love for the college game and all it embraces. For one more year, at least, he would rather experience the thrill of running through the 'T' at Neyland Stadium than trotting out onto the field at a concrete municipal ballpark in Philadelphia or Oakland.

"He chose the traditional Walk to the Stadium down Yale Avenue [now "Peyton Manning Pass"] in preference to riding in a limousine to the scene of Sunday afternoon's NFL encounter. Pregame, a pep rally on campus over sitting around a hotel Saturday night in downtown Baltimore. Postgame, a leisurely family dinner at a Knoxville steakhouse over a transcontinental flight back from Seattle.

"Peyton relishes the entire college scene—studying game film with David Cutcliffe, heeding Bud Ford's call to do just one more interview, calling the toss of the coin as a Vol captain, meeting kids at Fan's Day in the spring, talking over the game plan at midweek with Phillip Fulmer, hobnobbing with Tennessee followers in the hotel lobby Saturday morning on the road."

We fast forward to January 1998, when Manning was named an NCAA Top VIII recipient, a national award recognizing student–athletes from the preceding calendar year for their athletic accomplishments, academic achievement, character, and leadership. Manning was the first Tennessee athlete chosen for the Top VIII Award capping not only his overall career at Tennessee but also a period from that day in March 1997 when he delighted all of Big Orange Coun-

Peyton accepts the James E. Sullivan Award at Thompson–Boling Arena in Knoxville. ▶

▲ *Jamal Lewis, who solidified the Vol running attack in 1997 with 1364 yards, struggles ahead for yardage.*

▲ *Peyton never refuses an autograph request.*

try by choosing to return for his senior season as a Vol instead of turning pro. His decision to stay at UT was universally hailed as a definitive statement on behalf of college football and the true importance of what it means to be a student–athlete.

It was a dazzling time for the second son of Archie and Olivia Manning, who had to have impressed everyone who saw him with his impassioned love for college football and the poise and polish he displayed under the relentless media attention that was thrust upon him his senior season and, when you think about it, during his entire collegiate career.

Who could forget that memorable December 1997 night on "The David Letterman Show" when Manning matched the CBS personality one-liner for one-liner and tossed a football through a second story window outside the Ed Sullivan Studio, then witnessed Letterman do likewise?

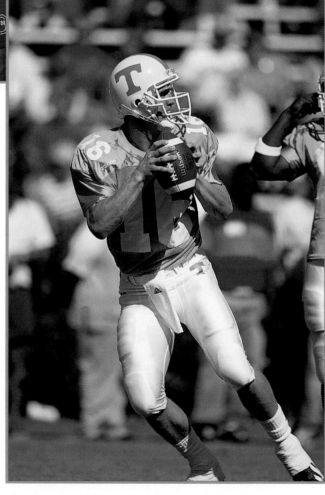

▲ *Peyton is dangerous with the football in his hand and Vol receivers in the vicinity.*

▲ *General Neyland's game maxims talk about gang-tackling. A South Carolina running back finds out first-hand.*

Manning was chosen to give the acceptance speech on behalf of the Top VIII Award winners on January 11 and here's a portion of what he said:

"Eight of us . . . eight student–athletes are here to be honored for the significant and often difficult choices we made throughout our college years . . . decisions and ramifications that often set us apart from our classmates and from our teammates. It is traditional to thank the NCAA for this honor. However, I would rather not. What I believe is more appropriate is to thank our institutions and all of you for the opportunity to play intercollegiate athletics and for the life lessons they taught us.

"It is popular today to ask with derision if big-time college sports are even compatible with higher education. The critics ask if athletics is consistent with the educational mission of colleges and universities. Frankly, those people see the walls that limit us, without seeing the spaces that allow us to expand.

"The reality is that collegiate sports have a lot more to do with learning than they do with winning. As student–athletes, we have learned more than most people about the blessings and lasting pleasure of camaraderie and shared sacrifice, collective responsibility and commitment to excellence, and both time management and life management.

"It would have been a lot easier to have been a football player and not just a student, and, conversely, it would have been much easier to have just been a student and left the football for some other day and time. But it wouldn't have been as joyous, as rich, or quite candidly, as humbling to have been one without the other. I would bet you that each and every one of tonight's honorees would say without hesitation that he or she is a better man or woman and a better leader because of those experiences.

"So for all of us, I say thank you from the bottom of my heart, not for a single award on a single night,

Peyton meets the media after a big win.

but for the many memorable and molding moments that we have had the privilege to call ourselves student–athletes."

The memories of Peyton Manning are rich and full, ones to be savored for a lifetime. He was always there to sign one more autograph or visit one more youngster. He always spoke in the hallway. Always. He was a joy to be around.

In the spring of 1997, he was among 75 UT students who were selected to the Epsilon Chapter of Phi Beta Kappa, honoring "outstanding academic achievement in the pursuit of a broadly based liberal arts education." (Candidates come from the top 10 percent of their graduating class, with superlative GPAs, intermediate-level competence in a foreign language, a specific level of mathematics, a junior or senior standing, and a two-year minimum residency at Tennessee being required.)

Peyton was treasurer of Pi Eta Lambda Honor Society for Speech Communication, a member of the Unity Council, limited to 12 players who serve as a liaison between the football team and the coaching staff, and the Student–Athlete Advisory Committee, an Athletic Department Committee made up from representatives from all sports.

In the community, he was chairman of the 1996 Multiple Sclerosis Read-A-Thon and was featured in the *Knoxville News-Sentinel* reading to children at A.L. Lotts Elementary School from the book *Be a Perfect Person in Just Three Days*, complete with a necklace of broccoli around his neck.

Peyton was a featured speaker, along with U.S. Senator Bill Frist (R-Tennessee), when 300 of the top students from public, private, and parochial schools across East Tennessee were honored at Knoxville's Hyatt Regency Hotel. He worked at the Knoxville Boys and Girls Club and has been deeply involved in the Fellowship of Christian Athletes, speaking at the organization's annual fund-raising breakfasts. He had an internship with Knoxville's Downtown Organization. He spoke at a Campus Leadership Conference in 1996.

He gave his personal testimony at Lincoln Memorial University in Harrogate, Tennessee, with over 1,000 people in attendance, and was the guest speaker for two first-year studies classes on the importance of time management and good study habits. He volunteered at Lakeshore Mental Health Institute and was grand marshall of Knoxville's annual Dogwood Arts Parade.

In one of his unique experiences, Peyton spoke at graduation ceremonies at the Morgan County Regional Correction Facility near Wartburg, Tennessee, calling it "truly a good experience."

"It opens your eyes to the world a little more," he said. "Any time you go to a place like that, you learn you don't want to go back for the wrong reasons. It makes you think twice about some things you're tempted to do, because you never know what might happen.

"There were some nice people in there, but obviously they had done something wrong in their lives. It makes you want to hang around the right people."

On the field, he is the holder of 33 school records. He holds the NCAA records for the lowest interception percentage for a season and career. He was a three-time finalist for the Heisman Trophy, finishing second in 1997.

It was at that nationally televised Heisman ceremony that Peyton showcased exactly who he is and what he stood for. It was indicative of Peyton Manning's character that he was the first to congratulate Michigan's Charles Woodson when the 1997 Heisman Trophy winner was announced December 13 in New York City. If you knew Peyton, you wouldn't have expected any less. But there's more to the story.

"Long after Heisman Trophy winner Charles Woodson of Michigan departed into a cold, windy night near the World Trade Center, long after other Heisman candidates Ryan Leaf of Washington State and Randy Moss of Marshall were gone," former *Knoxville News-Sentinel* reporter Jimmy Hyams wrote, "there Peyton Manning stood, answering countless questions and obliging autograph-seekers when you knew he'd rather be somewhere else."

He topped the 300-yard passing mark 18 times in his career, including seven straight games. He is the "winningest" quarterback in SEC history, with a 39–5 record as a starter. In 1996, Manning became the first Tennessee quarterback to throw for more than 3,000 yards in a single season and duplicated that feat in 1997. A Johnny Unitas Award winner as the nation's top quarterback, Peyton was named the 1997 SEC Player of the Year after having been the 1994 SEC Freshman of the Year.

But statistics don't tell the whole story, even if John Borton of *Wolverine Watch*, an independent newsletter covering the University of Michigan, declared Peyton to be "statistically corpulent." (That, friends, is a two-dollar word for "overburdened.") Peyton is the real deal, just what you want in a college athlete—the athlete media types and fans in general clamor for yet don't fully appreciate.

When Peyton walked across the Thompson–Boling Arena stage on May 16, 1997, as a graduate of the UT Class of 1997, he might have been better known had he worn his Orange jersey with No. 16 on the front, back, and shoulders, and the name "Manning" emblazoned thereon. He chose, however, the requisite cap and gown for the College of Arts and Sciences, complete with a medal awarded by his major area of study, Speech Communication. He graduated cum laude, carrying a 3.6 GPA. He was the department's No. 1 graduate, graduating a year ahead of his class.

"It was tough and definitely challenging," he said of his three-year undergraduate career. "This past semester's been tough, since I was taking 22 hours. I didn't have any intentions of getting done in three years. My high school, Isidore Newman High School in New Orleans, taught me good study habits and how to organize my time.

"One thing that helped me was coming in and playing so early. I got in here and was thrown into the fire. That helped me organize my football time and my school time as well. I maintained a good GPA my freshman year and carried it on through."

He has already joined the list of legendary Vol players of the past, as Vol fans speak of him in the same reverential tones they reserve for men like Gene McEver,

Bobby Dodd, Bob Suffridge, Hank Lauricella, Doug Atkins, John Majors, Dewey Warren, Bob Johnson, Condredge Holloway, Reggie White, Heath Shuler, and many, many others. His accomplishments are the staple of conversation wherever Vol fans gather, at alumni meetings or in barbershops or court squares, from Copper Basin to Union City, Hohenwald to Hartsville, Memphis to Bristol. There is still a great discussion about his impromptu TD runs against Alabama in 1995 and Vanderbilt in 1997, plays on which Peyton appeared to hand the ball off to a diving tailback, only to keep it and sprint to his left for the score on what the football intelligentsia call the "naked reverse."

Mothers and dads have named their children after him and the Knoxville Zoo likewise has a giraffe named Peyton. A campus thoroughfare is named after him, with Yale Avenue being renamed "Peyton Manning Pass" this past winter. There is a University Scholarship Fund named in his honor and his jersey has been retired, a hot topic this past March and April on the local talk shows. He was honored at halftime of the 1998 Orange and White game, as Vol fans came to their feet as one, saying "thanks for the memories" one more time.

▲ *Co-captain Leonard Little (1) was the leader of the Vol defense.*

▲ *Peyton discusses football with young quarterbacks.*

He was the National Football Foundation's National Scholar–Athlete of the Year and received an NCAA postgraduate scholarship. When he received the Vincent dePaul Draddy Award December 9, here's a portion of what he said: "I came to these ceremonies when I was 12 years old when my dad was inducted into the College Football Hall of Fame. That night, he said, 'Football is not about glory; it's about dreams.' Everyone here has one thing in common: college football. I have had four wonderful years at the University of Tennessee academically, athletically, and personally."

He visits local hospitals and schools on a regular basis. He has been an active member of the D.A.R.E. program and has participated in public service announcements urging young people to stay in school and to wear bicycle helmets.

There are some final things even the most casual observer of Peyton Manning notices quickly. These are a definite sense of focus, a definite sense of priorities, and a definite sense of purpose.

▲ *Manning accepts the plaudits of the crowd at Thompson–Boling Arena.*

"I have preached on the importance of making faith, family, education, and social life priorities, in that order," Peyton said. "Hopefully, the students will understand that football is only a fraction of my life and I rank it along with my social responsibilities.

"I believe that I have successfully impacted at least a few students, hopefully more, but if I can help change even one student from drugs, violence, or other problems, I consider what I've done a success."

Peyton also has made a positive impression on one of his teachers. "There is another Peyton Manning," Faye Julian, professor of Speech Communication and Associate Dean, Undergraduate Affairs, said, "who is just as impressive, although not as well publicized. That Peyton is a warm, generous, and scholarly young man who does well in the classroom and serves his university and community.

"What most people don't know about Peyton is how willing he is to give of himself. He seemingly never turns down a chance to give a speech or read a book at a local school, or visit a church, or lend his name to charitable activities on campus. He is active in speech department activities, in campus events, and community causes. Blessed with enormous talent and poise, he is humble, kind, and caring."

It was former Vol fullback Curt Watson (1969–71), talking with Archie Manning on the phone one day, who put all of this into perspective. There was no way to tell what Archie said in response, but Curt won-dered if Archie, who played quarterback for Ole Miss from 1968–70 and literally took apart an undefeated Vol 11 in a 38–0 win in 1969, ever considered back in those days that nearly 30 years later a younger Manning would be such a hero in Knoxville, Tennessee, of all places.

Time, of course, was a great healer. Peyton is now the toast of Big Orange Country, and Archie and Olivia Manning have enjoyed it more than anybody. Peyton was a co-captain of the 1997 squad and has an SEC Championship ring as a lasting memory of the season he came back to enjoy.

There is no doubt that Peyton Manning has made Tennesseans proud. There's no doubt that he has been a credit to the University of Tennessee. He's earned the respect of Vol fans and has contributed to the Volunteer legend. When all is said and done, that's a great legacy.

He was a "can't miss prospect" who didn't. Russ Bebb, the author of two books on Tennessee football, said, "He is the most popular athlete to ever play any sport in Tennessee history. He is head and shoulders above anybody else. I like to refer to him as the Jimmy Stewart of college football. He just represents everything good about the game."

His name is Peyton Manning and this is his story.

—Knoxville, Tennessee
April 1998

TENNESSEE FOOTBALL: THE HISTORICAL PERSPECTIVE

When you talk about Tennessee football, you're talking about tradition. Tradition is a wonderful thing, particularly the storied tradition of Tennessee football. You can't manufacture it and nobody really knows how to define it, but you know it when you see it. And, perhaps, more importantly, you know it when you feel it.

Tennessee tradition is a distinctive shade of Orange (PMS 021 for the purists), unmatched anywhere in college football. It's the T's on the sides of the helmet. It's the "Vol Walk" down "Peyton Manning Pass" (*nee* Yale Avenue) from Gibbs Hall to Neyland Stadium. It's the Orange and White checkerboard end zones. It's a wave of Orange across the expanse of Neyland Stadium, or for that matter, wherever the Vols play.

It's tailgating in the parking lots and hearing and seeing John Ward and Bill Anderson's pre-game "Kickoff Call-in Show" at the base of the Hill near Alumni Memorial Gym. It's hearing Bobby Denton say, "Please Pay These Prices and Please Pay No More." It's watching the "Pride of the Southland Marching Band," marching down Volunteer Boulevard, turning right on Andy Holt, and heading to Stadium Drive.

Tennessee tradition is the band massed at the north end, ready to begin the nation's most exciting pre-game show, culminating when the Vols run through the "T." It's "Rocky Top," "The Spirit of the Hill," and "The University of Tennessee Alma Mater," complete with solo trumpet. It's the Volunteer Navy, on Fort Loudon Lake, with boats there of all sizes and descriptions.

The team that makes the fewest mistakes will win.

Play for and make the breaks, and when one comes your way—Score!

If at first the game, or breaks, go against you, don't let up. Put on more steam.

Protect our kickers, our QB, our lead, and our ball game.

Ball, oskie, cover, block, cut and slice, pursue, and gang tackle . . . for this is the winning edge.

Press the kicking game. Here is where the breaks are made.

Carry the fight to our opponent and keep it there for 60 minutes.

—The Robert R. Neyland Game Maxims

Part of Tennessee tradition are the "T's" on the sides of the helmets.

When Peyton Manning signed on with the Vols in February 1994, he hooked on with one of the most tradition-rich programs in the nation, a program which dates to 1891 and has 17 members in the College Football Hall of Fame. The Vols are 677–286–53 over that time and have been a major force in college football.

Robert Reese Neyland had not yet been born when the Vols played their first football game in November 1891 and over 100 years of football tradition were begun. But remember the name.

Peyton Manning has joined the storied tradition of the "greats" . . . the

The "Pride of the Southland Marching Band" is an integral part of Tennessee tradition.

players, coaches, and fans, the people who have helped build the program. From Bob Neyland to Phillip Fulmer, from Gene McEver to Bob Johnson, from Nathan Washington Dougherty to Reggie White. And all points in between. Young men in Orange have ranged across the gridiron, wherever the gridiron, giving their all for Tennessee. It's like former fullback Leonard Coffman (1937–39) once said: "To play for Tennessee, you have to get wet all over."

The Vols' debut on the gridiron in that 1891 season was none too promising, as Sewanee defeated the Vols, 24–0, in a game played in the muck and mire in Chattanooga. It was also the only game on that year's schedule. The results of the game, it should be noted, were not reported until four days later. The record also shows that Neyland was born a few months later, on February 17, 1892, in Greenville, Texas, and his influence on the Vol program would be felt from 1926 on, even through today.

The first win would come in 1892, a 25–0 decision at Maryville. The first home win would have to wait until 1893, as the Vols topped Maryville again, this time by 32–0.

THE FORMATIVE YEARS: A NEW STADIUM IS BUILT IN 1921

In the early years, between 1891 and 1911, football coaches came and went, frequently on a year-to-year basis. The Vols did not have a head coach until 1899 (J. A. Pierce was the first), and had seven head coaches between that time and 1911. One coach, George Levene (1907–09), came with the personal recommendation of the legendary Walter Camp. The negotiations for Levene's services went on largely by mail and were conducted by team manager David C. Gaut.

In the 1907 season, organized cheerleading was brought to the campus by R. C. (Red) Matthews.

The Vols won the 1914 Southern Intercollegiate Athletic Association championship under head coach Zora Clevenger, piling up 374 points to 37 for their opponents. They also were the first Vol squad to defeat Vanderbilt, doing so 16–14 on November 7. In 1916, the first Homecoming game was held, as the Vols again defeated Vanderbilt 10–6.

▲ *Vol cheerleaders help increase spirit at Tennessee games.*

▲ *Vol wide receivers celebrate a 1997 Citrus Bowl touchdown.*

Drive) and was named for its benefactors, Knoxville banker and UT trustee William S. Shields and his wife, Alice Watkins Shields. It opened that season with 3,200 seats, although it had been used for baseball the previous spring.

A year later, in 1922, the Vols wore Orange jerseys for the first time (black shirts with Orange and White piping had been the previous color of choice), taking the color from the common American Daisy which grew in profusion on the Hill just north of the stadium. A Vol guard of 1922–23 vintage, Estes Kefauver of Madisonville, became a United States Senator and was a candidate for Vice President in 1956. Rufe Clayton scored the first TD on Shields–Watkins Field on an 11-yard run and the Vols pitched shutouts in all four games played in their new home.

In 1925, the Beer Barrel was introduced as the prize for the winner of the Tennessee–Kentucky game and has been so ever since. In its early days, it was painted with the words "Ice Water" to satisfy the local temper-

It was not until 1920, 29 years into the program's history, that the Vols won their 100th game, a 49–0 victory over Transylvania. The leading player of that time was Nathan Washington Dougherty, an All-Southern selection in 1907 and 1908, and known to his teammates as "Big-Un." He was later inducted into the College Football Hall of Fame in 1967.

Tennessee had played its games on Wait Field at the corner of 15th Street and Cumberland Avenue on campus, but moved into a new home in 1921. Shields–Watkins Field was less than a mile away on 15th Street (now Stadium

▲ *Trey Teague, Corey Terry, and Bill Duff (L-R) bring home the famed "Beer Barrel" after a win over Kentucky.*

ance unions. Today it rests with the winning team of the previous year's contest, Tennessee since 1985.

The 1925 season saw head coach M. B. Banks fall ill the week of the Georgia game—October 31. Neyland and fellow assistant coach Bunny Oakes took command of the squad and hit the Bulldogs with a neat piece of gamesmanship. Neyland claimed Georgia used an illegal shift and announced he would prove it with pictures taken during the game. Georgia coaches had Bulldog supporters working overtime to block the camerman's view of the field. The kickoff was delayed when the train bringing the officials to the game was late and the contest finished in rain and virtual darkness. The Vols won 12–7 in one of the great efforts of the early years of Tennessee football.

ENTER BOB NEYLAND: A TRADITION IS BORN

Banks resigned as head coach on December 17, 1925, and went to Knoxville's Central High School. In 1926, Neyland, then an ROTC instructor, Army captain, and backfield coach the previous season, was named head coach and served through the end of the 1934 season when the Army beckoned him to Panama. Dougherty, a dean of UT's College of Engineering and longtime faculty chairman of athletics, had hired Neyland in 1926 with the injunction: *"Even the score with Vanderbilt; do something about our terrible standing in the series."*

The Vols trailed the Commodores in the series 2–17–2 after the 1925 season. When Neyland stepped down 26 years later, the ledger with the Commodores was dead even at 21–21–4. Neyland himself was 16–3–2 against Vanderbilt. By any measure you want, Neyland "did something" about the series.

In 1926, 3,600 seats were added to the east side of Shields–Watkins Field and the Vols of that season dispatched eight opponents, six by shutouts. Allyn McKeen scored the first touchdown of the Neyland era, picking up his own fumble and scoring from 11 yards out. Later in that season, Jimmy Elmore, elected Mayor of Knoxville in the years to come, returned a dropkick 95 yards for a score against Carson-Newman and earned a lecture from Neyland for doing so.

The Vols won the Southern Conference championship in 1927 with an 8–0–1 record, the first undefeated season since 1916, and looked forward to the 1928 season. The Vols freshman team that season, known locally as the "Rats," went undefeated, outscoring their opponents by 160–14. In that 1928 season, the Vols defeated heavily favored Alabama, 15–13, in Tuscaloosa, as tailback Gene McEver, the "Bristol Blizzard" and one of the "Flaming Sophomores of 1928," took the opening kickoff 98 yards for a score. It was the run and the game that catapulted Tennessee into the college football business to stay. Football historians note that Neyland went to Alabama coach Wallace Wade and requested to shorten the game

▲ *Neyland Stadium/Shields–Watkins Field has been the "Home of the Vols" since 1921.*

▲ *The "VOLS" sign dominates the south end of Neyland Stadium.*

if events warranted. As events turned out, it wasn't necessary.

Buddy Hackman did likewise with the opening kickoff a week later against Washington & Lee and the Vol express was off and running. Hackman and McEver became known as the "Touchdown Twins." The Vol backfield was popularly known as "Hack, Mack, and Dodd." The 1928 season also saw the UT Alma Mater selected in a contest sponsored by the UT Men's Glee Club. In 1929, McEver became Tennessee's first All-America selection, a year he led the nation in scoring with 130 points.

The win over Vanderbilt in Nashville had an interesting background. Despite having a game against Carson-Newman on November 9, Neyland took 10 Vol first-teamers with him to Nashville to watch the Commodores against Georgia Tech. The unorthodox scouting trip must have worked. The Vols who stayed home defeated Carson-Newman by 73–0, while the next week, the reconstituted varsity won over Vandy by 13–0. The 1929 season also saw the addition of 42 rows and 11,069 seats to the stadium's west side.

Bobby Dodd was an All-America selection in 1930, with the famed sportswriter Grantland Rice saying of him: *"In his three years at Tennessee, he figured in just one losing game and on any number of occasions his keen directing strategy saved the day."* Tennessee played in its first bowl game in 1931, a 13–0 victory over New York University in the New York Charity Game at Yankee Stadium. Vol lineman Herman Hickman had an outstanding game that afternoon and Rice added Hickman to his All-America team on the basis of that performance.

Tennessee won the Southern Conference championship again in 1932 with an 9–0–1 record and joined the fledgling Southeastern Conference a year later. The 1932 season was marked by a 7–3 win over Alabama at Legion Field in Birmingham, highlighted by a kicking duel in the rain between Beattie Feathers and Alabama's John Cain that was without parallel in Vol history. Feathers kicked it 23 times and Cain kicked it 19. Feathers led the SEC in scoring in 1933 and was named All-America. In 1934, Tennessee won its 200th game, defeating Mississippi in Knoxville.

Leonard Little bears down on Georgia quarterback Mike Bobo.

Between 1926 and 1934, Neyland and the Vols had assembled a 76–7–5 record, with undefeated streaks of 33 and 28 games along with a 14-game winning streak. McEver was the first Vol inducted into the College Football Hall of Fame (1954). Feathers (1955), Dodd (1959), and Hickman (1959) followed McEver into the College Hall of Fame. Neyland, for his part, was inducted in 1956. Dodd was also inducted into the College Hall of Fame in 1993 as a coach for his tenure and success at Georgia Tech.

NEYLAND RETURNS FROM PANAMA FOR THE SECOND OF HIS THREE GREAT ERAS

Bill Britton had taken Neyland's place in the 1935 season. Neyland returned home for the 1936 season and immediately began building another dynasty. The 1936 season saw a 70-yard punt return by Red Harp that keyed a 15–13 win over Duke. The 1936 Vols finished 17th in the inaugural Associated Press poll.

By 1938, he was ready. With another group of sensational sophomores leading the way, he began a three-year run in which the Vols won 30 consecutive regular season games and visited the Orange, Rose, and Sugar Bowls. Neyland was obviously ready for the 1938 season, as spring practice, if that is the proper word, started on January 9 and continued through mid-April. It must have worked because the Vols won the SEC title not only in 1938, but also in 1939 and 1940.

The 1938 team ended with an 11–0 record, defeating Oklahoma in the 1939 Orange Bowl, while the 1939 team shut out 10 consecutive opponents. No Vol team has gone 11–0 since like the 1938 bunch did and no collegiate team has since shut out an entire slate of opponents like the 1939 team. From the second quar-

The "Tennessee Walking Horse" is as much a part of Tennessee football as Orange jerseys and Shields–Watkins Field.

ter of the LSU game on October 29, 1938, it would be 17 games and 71 quarters, well into the 1940 regular season, before a Vol opponent scored again. Were these guys good on defense or what?

The Vols brought home a check for $100,000 from the 1940 Rose Bowl. Sophomore guard Bob Suffridge earned the first of three All-America honors during his career in 1938, becoming the Vols' only three-time All-America selection. Also in 1938, Shields–Watkins Field (sometimes referred to in this era as Shields–Watkins Stadium) was expanded on the east side by 44 rows and 10,030 seats to a capacity of 31,390 seats.

In the 1939 Alabama game, which found Ted Husing of CBS and Bill Stern of NBC at Shields–Watkins Field covering the game, a sophomore tailback from Knoxville named Johnny Butler etched his name into Vol history with a 56-yard run against the Tide, on which he went sideline to sideline for the score untouched by Tide tacklers. The Vols were ranked No. 1 on October 24 that season, holding the No. 1 spot for four weeks, through November 14. It is still a mystery to many long-time Vol fans how a team that is unscored on in the regular season was not named national champion.

Neyland's record during this era was 43–7–3. Players from that era inducted into the College Football Hall of Fame were Suffridge (1961), guard Ed Molinski (1990), tailback George Cafego (1969), and end Bowden Wyatt (inducted as a player in 1972 and as a coach in 1997).

After the 1940 season, however, Neyland was called back to the military as winds of war hovered over the world. He was gone until the 1946 season, leaving the Vol football program in the capable hands of John Barnhill, who later became head coach and

▲ *There are always fireworks at Neyland Stadium, either during the game or at halftime during the band show.*

athletic director at Arkansas. Barnhill compiled a 32–5–2 record and led the Vols to the Sugar and Rose Bowls. The Vols also played their first night game in 1944, a 13–0 decision at LSU.

Four Vol players did not return home from World War II. They were Bill Nowling (32), Rudy Klarer (49), Willis Tucker (61), and Clyde "Ig" Fuson (62). They are memorialized in the Tennessee Hall of Fame Exhibit on campus. Their numbers have been retired by the University.

Neyland's Final Years: A National Championship Comes to Knoxville

Neyland arrived home from World War II for the 1946 season, saying, "It will take us five years to put Tennessee back on top." The Vols immediately won the SEC Championship and a bid to the Orange Bowl. His dominant player that season was Dick Huffman, still remembered as one of the toughest Vols ever. He would lead the charge against Alabama quarterback Harry Gilmer in a 12–0 Vol win. Walter Slater had a 78-yard punt return to defeat North Carolina and Charley "Choo-Choo" Justice.

Critics argued that Neyland had lost his touch, particularly in view of 5–5 and 4–4–2 seasons in 1947 and 1948 and the assertion that his beloved single-wing offense had gone out of style. In 1948, Tennessee won its 300th game, defeating Alabama, 21–6, on Homecoming afternoon. By the end of 1948, Neyland was ready for his final run as Vol head man. He did so in an expanded arena, with Shields–Watkins Field being expanded that year at the south end, with 15,000 seats making the new capacity 46,390. It was just before the 1949 season that Vol publicist Lindsey Nelson (later NBC's, the New York Mets', and Notre Dame's) formed the first Vol Radio Network.

After a 7–2–1 mark in 1949, led by another talented group of sophomores, the likes of Bert Rechichar, Gordon Polofsky, Hank Lauricella, Bob Davis, and their talented rookie teammates, the Vols kicked off the decade of the 1950s with an 11–1 season, marred only by a 7–0 loss at Mississippi State in the season's second week. The Vols rolled through the rest of the season and upset Texas in the 1951 Cotton Bowl, sparked by a 75-yard run by tailback Hank Lauricella that Stern called one of the best he had ever seen. Other than the Cotton Bowl, the highlight game of the season was a 7–0 win over Kentucky in the snow on Shields–Watkins Field. The game was broadcast on the Liberty Broadcasting Network and featured Nelson on the play-by-play. It was Nelson's national broadcast debut and a key moment in his professional career.

Neyland's 1951 team came back and won the national championship with a 10–0 regular season record. The contest with Alabama that season, a 27–13 Vol victory, was the Vols' first on a new invention called television. The Vols' best performance that season may have been the 28–0 win over Kentucky at Stoll Field in Lexington, as Lauricella once again outdueled Kentucky's Babe Parilli. Lauricella, that season's Heisman Trophy runner-up, and defensive tackle Doug Atkins were later named to the College Football Hall of Fame, in 1981 and 1985, respectively. Atkins, named also to the Pro Football Hall of Fame for his work at Cleveland, Chicago, and New Orleans, is the only Vol enshrined in both. He was also named SEC "Player of the Quarter Century" in 1976. In 1996, guard John Michels, who found fame as an assistant with the Minnesota Vikings, was likewise inducted into the College Hall of Fame. Fullback Andy Kozar, now Dr. Andy Kozar, was named the winner of the NCAA Silver Anniversary Award in 1977, honoring his accomplishments 25 years after he left UT.

Tennessee finished with an 8–2–1 record in 1952, but the big story was Neyland stepping down as the Vol head coach just before the Cotton Bowl game against Texas, a game the Vols lost, 16–0. His record for his third stint at Tennessee was 54–17–4 and his overall record was 173–31–12.

It was in 1953 that Smokey, a blue-tick coon hound, became the Vols' official mascot by vote of the student body. There have been Smokeys ever since, eight in all, provided by the Brooks and Hudson families of Knoxville.

Harvey Robinson became the Vols' new head coach in 1953, serving through the 1954 season. The 1954 season marked the debut of a young tailback from Huntland named John Majors, who had a 79-yard

Going into 1998, Phillip Fulmer was the nation's winningest active coach.

run leading the Vols to a 19–7 victory over Mississippi State at Crump Stadium in Memphis. The Vols were 4–2 entering November, but lost their final four games. Neyland called dismissing Robinson after that season "the hardest thing I've ever had to do."

1955: BOWDEN WYATT RETURNS HOME

Wyatt, who had been head coach at Wyoming and Arkansas, returned to campus as Vol head coach in 1955, 17 years after leading the Vols to an 11–0 record in 1938. He hit the jackpot in 1956, his second year, as the Vols won the SEC and earned a berth in the Sugar Bowl. The Vols' 6–0 win over Georgia Tech that No-vember, matching Neyland protégés Wyatt and Dodd at Atlanta's Grant Field, was later voted the second greatest college football game of all time. It was a masterpiece of field position football as taught by Gen. Neyland. When Dodd punted from the Vol 28 in the first quarter of a scoreless game, Wyatt was asked after the game why Dodd didn't go for it. Wyatt's answer was simple: "He wouldn't have made it." Johnny Majors took nearly every award that season, but finished second to Notre Dame's Paul Hornung in the Heisman Trophy voting, a decision which rankles Vol fans to this day. For his part, Majors was inducted into the College Football Hall of Fame in 1987.

The Vols followed up the 1956 season with an 8–3 season in 1957 and played Bear Bryant's last Texas A&M team in the Gator Bowl, winning 3–0 on the ac-

▲ *There's nothing like the spirit of Tennessee football at Neyland Stadium.*

▲ *You know it's football time in Tennessee when the Vols run through the giant "T" just before game time at Neyland Stadium.*

curate toe of placekicker Sammy Burklow. The game featured a memorable collision between Vol tailback Bobby Gordon and A&M's Heisman Trophy winner John David Crow. Both were dazed on the play, but each returned to action.

The 1958 season was a mixed bag. The Vols lost to Auburn 13–0 in the season opener and didn't make a first down all day. They did defeat Bear Bryant's first Alabama team by 14–7 and knocked Ole Miss out of the Cotton Bowl with an 18–16 win on Homecoming. The Vols were also surprised when Florida State and Chattanooga scored upset wins in Knoxville.

The Vols closed out the decade with two major upset victories in 1959, defeating Auburn 3–0 in September and LSU 14–13 in November, both games in Knoxville. The LSU game featured the Vols stopping LSU Heisman Trophy winner Billy Cannon at the goal when the Tigers, trailing 14–13, went for two midway

in the fourth quarter. Bill Majors, Charley Severance, and Wayne Grubb were present and voting on the game's pivotal play.

The 1960 season saw the Vols begin the decade with a 10–3 win over Auburn in Birmingham and a 20–7 triumph over Alabama in Knoxville. No one knew that the Vols would not defeat the Tigers again until 1966 and the Tide until 1967. The Vols went 6–2–2 that season and 6–4 in 1961.

On March 28, 1962, Gen. Neyland died in New Orleans. In his memory, the stadium was named "Neyland Stadium" and an academic scholarship fund started, both events happening at the Alabama game. There was a new upper deck seating 5,837 on the west side, plus a new press box, making total stadium capacity 52,227.

Wyatt's tenure as Vol coach ended after a 4–6 record in 1962, with assistant coach Jim McDonald

Did anyone say "Defense!, Defense!" Vol defenders, like Al Wilson,
Tyrone Hines, and Bill Duff, have always answered the call.

taking the reins for the 1963 season. The schedule-maker did Wyatt no favors in that 1962 season, as the Vols played the first three games of the season on the road and made their home debut against defending national champ Alabama.

During the 1963 season, the first Neyland Stadium crowd over 50,000 saw the Vols play Georgia Tech. Later that season, the Vols took their 400th victory, defeating Tulane, 26–0, in New Orleans. McDonald attacked the Vol job with a zealot's fervor and had the right spirit, but too few horses by several to attack the 1963 slate of opponents. Times were changing in Knoxville and by the end of 1963 a bold move had taken place in the Vol football program. It began in late November and early December.

DOUG DICKEY BRINGS THE "T" FORMATION TO KNOXVILLE

After the 1963 season, Doug Dickey, then a top assistant to Frank Broyles at Arkansas, became the Vols' head coach, bringing the "T" formation with him to Knoxville. Dickey had played for AD Bob Woodruff at Florida in the early 1950s. Dickey's first Tennessee team finished 4–5–1, but hopes were high as the Vols narrowly lost to Auburn and Alabama (a game marked by a tenacious goal-line stand at the north end), tied LSU at Baton Rouge, and upset favored Georgia Tech at Grant Field. Middle guard Steve DeLong won the

▲ *John Ward (left) and Bill Anderson (right), having called the story of Tennessee football on the Vol Network since 1968, will make the 1998 season their last.*

▲ *Jonathan Brown, a part of the 1994 recruiting class, made life miserable for opposing quarterbacks.*

Outland Trophy and Dickey's staff recruited a freshman class which would help lead the Vols out of the football wilderness. (DeLong was ultimately named to the College Football Hall of Fame in 1993. His brother, Ken, was a part of this 1964–65 class and his son, Keith, would be a Vol All-America 25 years later in 1988.)

One of that year's recruits, wide receiver Richmond Flowers from Montgomery, Alabama, was the first of a number of track–football athletes who brought a new dimension of speed to the Vol program. The 1964 season also saw the Vols move their bench to the west side of Shields–Watkins Field. In future years, the Vols would enter the arena through a giant "T" formed by the "Pride of the Southland Marching Band." It was a marvelous sight.

Dickey's second team finished 8–1–2 and earned a Bluebonnet Bowl bid, UT's first bowl game since 1957. The season's pivotal moment came in the aftermath of the Alabama game. The Vols had tied Alabama 7–7 at Birmingham's Legion Field on October 16, a game in which the Tide's Ken Stabler threw the ball away in the shadow of the Vol goal, thinking he had a down left for the game-winning field goal. He didn't, and the Vols came back to Knoxville having fought the favored Tide hammer and tong for 60 minutes. Spirits were high on the Knoxville campus. Line coach Charley Rash put a note in each of his linemen's mailbox that night after the game, saying: *"Play like that every week and you'll go undefeated."*

Two days later, Rash, Bill Majors (one of three Majors brothers to play at Tennessee), and Bob Jones, quarterback of the Baylor team that defeated the Vols 13–7 in the 1957 Sugar Bowl, were killed in an early morning car–train collision in West Knoxville. Even today, over 30 years later, many people connected with the Vol program still praise the way Dickey handled the tragedy, pulling everybody together and keeping the Vol program going. It was a key moment in Dickey's young coaching career.

One of the most memorable moments of that, or any other, season was the 37–34 "Rosebonnet Bowl" victory over UCLA at Memorial Stadium in Memphis, so named by Vol broadcaster George Mooney because of the post-season destinations of the two teams. It was a classic offensive shootout that was finally settled

▲ *Coach Fulmer leads the Vols onto the field at Kentucky.*

when Vol quarterback Dewey Warren ambled around left end for the winning score and Bobby Petrella grabbed a last-ditch Bruin aerial.

In 1966, there was an addition of 5,895 seats to the north stands, which increased stadium capacity to

58,122. There was also a new scoreboard at the north end, with a "countdown clock," replacing one that was really a clock, complete with minute and second hands. Tennessee's 8–3 record, including an 18–12 Gator Bowl win over a Syracuse team that featured Larry Csonka and Floyd Little, presaged what was to come in 1967. One memorable moment in that game came when linebacker Paul Naumoff hit Csonka head-on in a collision that could be heard across the stadium and another came later on when he ran down Little from behind when a touchdown appeared imminent. The Vols had four All-America selections (the most since 1939), Naumoff, tight end Austin Denney, punter Ron Widby, and center Bob Johnson.

The 1967 Vols lost their opener to UCLA, a nocturnal affair at the Los Angeles Memorial Coliseum, but came back to win their remaining nine games and the SEC Championship, earning an Orange Bowl date against Oklahoma. The Vols swept Alabama, Auburn, LSU, and Mississippi, defeating the Tide for the first time since 1960 and the Rebels for the first time since 1958, finishing No. 2 in the final polls. One other note: the Vols' 41–14 win over Vanderbilt in December was the last game played on the Neyland Stadium grass until September 1994.

Johnson, perhaps the Peyton Manning of his day, was a consensus All-America selection and was also an Academic All-America and a National Football Foundation Scholar–Athlete. He was selected to the College Football Hall of Fame in 1989 and won the NCAA Silver Anniversary Award in 1993.

In 1968, artificial turf came to Neyland Stadium. With the ersatz turf and the demise of the grass field came a 6,307-seat east upper deck and new auxiliary scoreboard, with the addition raising capacity to 64,429. John Ward and Bill Anderson took over the ra-

▲ *Coach Fulmer says Vol fans are No. 1 on a 1997 "Vol Walk" toward Neyland Stadium.*

dio broadcasts of Vol games that season and have been there ever since.

In the first game played on Tartan Turf against Vince Dooley's Georgia Bulldogs, Nashville's Lester McClain became the first black player to play in an SEC varsity football game. The Vols rallied for a 17–17 tie that day in an exciting finish led by quarterback Bubba Wyche. The Vols defeated Ole Miss 31–0, as a sophomore Rebel quarterback named Archie Manning—remember the name—had a hard day the week after the Vols had lost 28–14 to Auburn. Runner-up in the SEC in 1968, Tennessee won the crown again in 1969 with a 9–1 record and played in the Gator Bowl, highlighted by a 45–19 win over Auburn, a 41–14 pasting of Alabama at Legion Field, and a 17–3 win at Georgia. Manning and the Rebels turned the tables on the 7–0 Vols on November 15, as Ole Miss took a 38–0 decision at Jackson in a game that spoiled the Vols' national championship and big bowl dreams.

After the 1969 season, Dickey moved to Florida as head coach and 28-year-old Bill Battle became the Vols' new head man. His first team finished 11–1 and he became the first Division I head coach to win 11 games in his first year. Talk about your emotional season. During the 1970 season, Battle had to coach against the man who hired him in the Florida game and against his college coach in the Alabama game. The Vols won both games, two contests back-to-back as exciting as any in Vol history. Ole Miss wasn't on the schedule in 1970 or there might not have been enough season tickets to go around.

Seasons of 10–2 and 10–2 followed in 1971 and 1972. The 1971 team was known as the "offensive defense," as Vol defenders set NCAA records for most yards on interception returns (782), highest average per return (31.3 on 28 returns), and touchdowns off interceptions (seven). Jackie Walker had five TD returns off interceptions during his career. All are still NCAA

records. The Vols closed the 1971 regular season with a nationally televised 31–11 win over Penn State that shocked the nation and took a 14–13 win over Arkansas in the Liberty Bowl that didn't come easy.

In 1972, 6,221 seats were added to the stadium's southwest corner and capacity was increased to 70,650. The new seats were christened in the stadium's first night game, the home season opener against Penn State. The Vols won that night, 28–21, and night football became an integral part of the Vol tradition.

▲ *A quiet moment at Neyland Stadium for Vol coach Phillip Fulmer.*

In that 1972 season, Condredge Holloway became a whirling dervish under center, a master of the broken field run. He ran over, under, and even occasionally through opponents during his career, which saw him tabbed "The Artful Dodger." Coaches spent extra time trying to figure out how to stop him. Battle said that the only way to describe him was "indescribable." That word best describes some of Holloway's magic moves in the open field. Bowl seasons followed in 1973 and 1974. The Holloway magic may have best been exemplified on a two-point try that won the 1974 Clemson game. With the Vols trailing 28–27, Holloway rolled right at the south end, found all avenues blocked, and took the Great Circle Route back to his left toward the east side. Just when it appeared he would go down, he found Larry Seivers, a wide receiver from Clinton who was an All-America selection in 1975–76, for the game-winning points. Seivers' biggest problem was escaping the clutches of long-time Vol staffer Gus Manning after he made the game-winning catch.

In 1975, the Vols won their 500th game, defeating Kentucky, 17–13, at Commonwealth Stadium in Lexington. The 1975 team was also the first team in school history to draw over 500,000 fans (507,677) and the first to play in Hawaii.

A record crowd of 82,687 saw the Vols and Duke square off in the 1976 season opener and that large assemblage may have been the highlight. Battle resigned after the 1976 season and John Majors, then head coach of the national champion Pitt Panthers, answered the university's call, coming as head coach for the 1977 season. "Follow me to Tennessee" was the rallying cry. UT Chancellor Jack Reese had a masterpiece of understatement when he began the press conference announcing Majors' hire, by saying: "After an extensive nationwide search . . ."

JOHN MAJORS MARCHES HOME

His early teams had no bigger victory than a 40–18 win over Notre Dame in 1979, a season in which the Vols led eventual national champion Alabama 17–0 in the second quarter at Legion Field before losing. A 7–4 record was sufficient to earn a Bluebonnet Bowl bid.

A crowd of 95,288, swelled by an addition of permanent seating at the north end, saw the Vols and Georgia square off to begin the 1980 season. Georgia won 16–15, on its way to a national championship, unveiling a young tailback named Herschel Walker, but the Vols did have their moments that year, taking a 42–0 win at Auburn and concluding the season with a 45–14 win over Kentucky and a 51–13 win over Vanderbilt. The 1981 Vols overcame early, seemingly devastating, losses at Georgia and Southern Cal to post an 8–4 record and Garden State Bowl berth against Wisconsin. Slowly but surely, the Vols were on their way back.

With the 1982 World's Fair as a backdrop, Tennessee ended 11 years of frustration by defeating Alabama 35–28 at Neyland Stadium. Mike Terry's interception cinched things and Vol fans counted the clock down on the first of four consecutive wins over Alabama. The game would also mark Bryant's final Neyland Stadium appearance. He stepped down after the season and died the next January.

Placekicker Fuad Reveiz made his presence felt by kicking five field goals in each game in wins over Memphis State and Kentucky, and accounted for 33 points as the Vols won by 29–3 and 28–7, respectively. He had also kicked the game winner in a 23–21 win over Iowa State and had a 60-yarder against Georgia Tech. He was a late recruit in 1981. Vol assistant George Cafego called him "Frank," saying he was too old to learn to call him "Fuad."

Led by Reggie White, an absolute terror at defensive tackle, UT began an upsurge in fortunes in 1983, going 9–3 and winning the Florida Citrus Bowl. Johnnie Jones had the game-winner against the Tide, motoring 66 yards to break a 34–34 tie. That season, White had 15 sacks in leading the Vols up front. In 1984, the Vols rallied from a 27–13 deficit in the fourth quarter to defeat Alabama 28–27. Jones had his second straight 1,000-yard season and wideout Tim McGee finished his career with 123 catches, the best in Vol history to that time. Pete Panuska had a 100-yard kickoff return to highlight a Sun Bowl loss to Maryland.

In 1985, the Vols surprised everybody by defeating No. 1 Auburn 38–20, and Alabama 16–14, on their way to an SEC crown, the first since 1969, and a Sugar Bowl date with Miami. But it wasn't easy. Not at all.

Vol quarterback Tony Robinson, who had played brilliantly in a season-opening tie with UCLA and the win over Auburn, hurt a knee in the fourth quarter against Alabama and missed the rest of the season. Daryl Dickey, Doug Dickey's son, stepped into the breach and kept the Vol ship on course the rest of the way, including a 35–7 win over the Hurricanes that Vol fans remember fondly to this day. The Louisiana Superdome was "Big Orange Country South" that January 1, 1986, night. The 1986 team was 2–5 at one critical juncture, but won its last five games, including a 21–14 win in the Liberty Bowl against Minnesota.

UT won its season opener at the Meadowlands in 1987 in frantic and dramatic fashion, Phil Reich kicking a field goal in the final seconds to win over Iowa, 23–22. Vol linebacker Darrin Miller had a 96-yard return of a mid-air fumble. Almost immediately after the game, Reich earned a scholarship. Later that season, the Vols would trail Vanderbilt 28–3, but somehow win by 38–36.

When the Vols played Indiana at the Peach Bowl, Hoosier fans got their sports mixed up. When Reich missed a field goal at the end of the first half, and missed badly, we might add, shouts of "Air Ball!, Air Ball!" rang out from the Indiana faithful. The Vols had the last laugh, winning 27–22. The 1988 team won its last five games after an 0–6 start and things were looking up once again.

The 1989 season saw an 11–1 record, an SEC Championship and Cotton Bowl trip. The key game was in Week 2 when the Vols went to the Rose Bowl and soundly defeated UCLA 24–6. Tailback Chuck Webb had 294 yards rushing against Ole Miss and added 250 more in a 31–27 win over Arkansas in the Cotton Bowl. The win over Arkansas in Dallas on January 1, 1990, was the Vols' 600th. The Vols were the most improved team in the country, coming from 5–6 in 1988 to 1989's 11–1.

The 1990s began with another SEC championship and trip to the Sugar Bowl, with a come-from-behind 23–22 victory over Virginia. Webb was hurt in the second game and reserve tailback Tony Thompson came off the planks to amass 1261 yards and lead the SEC in rushing. Dale Carter keyed a 45–3 win over Florida with a 91-yard TD return off the second-half kickoff.

The Vols expanded a 7–3 halftime lead to win decisively by 45–3.

The highlight of the 1991 season came in South Bend, Indiana, at Notre Dame Stadium, when the Vols overcame a 31–7 deficit to somehow win by 35–34. Daryl Hardy's block of an Irish field goal attempt and Floyd Miley's return of the blocked kick for a score keyed the improbable comeback. John Becksvoort, Vol placekicker, had dreamed of defeating the Irish with a field goal, but, in this case, an extra point was plenty. The game went to the final seconds, with the Fighting Irish having a shot at the win, but misfiring on a last-second field goal, an attempt blocked by defensive back Jeremy Lincoln.

PHILLIP FULMER TAKES THE REINS OF THE VOL PROGRAM

The dominant story of the 1992 season was Majors' resignation and the promotion of Phillip Fulmer as the new head coach. While Majors recovered from heart surgery at UT Hospital, Fulmer, a Vol guard on teams from 1969–71, served as interim coach at the start of the season and the team notched three straight victories. Three straight losses in October proved pivotal and Majors resigned November 13, the night before the Vols' game with Memphis State. When Majors' resignation became effective at the end of the regular season, Dickey announced Fulmer's appointment as head coach prior to the Hall of Fame Bowl game with Boston College. A 38–23 victory over the Eagles brought down the curtain on a 9–3 worksheet. One highlight of the season was the election of former walk-on J. J. McCleskey as a team captain. The little guy (5' 8", 172) from Karns High School had 18 tackles against Alabama and ultimately made it to the NFL. It was quite a story.

Vol gridiron success continued through Fulmer's first full season as head coach. The Vols went 10–2 (with a tie against Alabama turned into a Vol win due to NCAA sanctions) in 1993, a year in which quarterback Heath Shuler finished runnerup for the Heisman Trophy. Tennessee was rewarded with a trip to

Phillip Fulmer relaxes in his Neyland–Thompson Sports Center Office.

the Florida Citrus Bowl where Penn State took a 31–13 victory.

In a media conference that January, just after the bowl game, Shuler announced that he was "following my dreams" and turning pro. He would play for the Washington Redskins and New Orleans Saints.

Peyton Manning signed on less than a month later and a new era of Tennessee football would begin, but no one could guess how quickly it would all begin to happen. That's where we begin, with the start of the 1994 season.

▲ *In varying sizes, Vol fans have been carrying the flag of Tennessee football for a number of years.*

PEYTON MANNING

THE PEYTON MANNING YEARS: NEW ORLEANS TO KNOXVILLE AND POINTS IN BETWEEN

On March 24, 1976, no one across the expanse of Big Orange Country could gaze 18 to 20 years into the future and see what impact the events of that day might have on Vol football fortunes from 1994 through 1997, even into 1998. No one was looking that far ahead. This is Tennessee football and the future is now.

All eyes were on head coach Bill Battle and what would happen to the Vols on the gridiron in 1976. On that March day, workmen were busying themselves with the addition of the remainder of the South Upper Deck, an addition of 9600 seats that would bring total stadium capacity to 80,250. Vol seniors were pictured on the front of the UT Press Guide with construction going on in the background.

That day, the *Knoxville News-Sentinel* carried a preview of the upcoming spring drills, complete with the likely starting lineups. Guard Mickey Marvin, free safety Mike Mauck, wingback Stanley Morgan, split end Larry Seivers, linebacker Andy Spiva, and safety Russ

> 66 *The Tennessee people through the generations have held loyalty and commitment in the very highest regard. Today we are blessed with the ultimate return of loyalty and commitment. This is truly a great day for Tennessee football and Peyton's decision makes a huge statement for Peyton Manning and his character, putting team and program, alumni and fans, and friends and teammates ahead of immediate financial gains and the limelight of the National Football League. Today, he totally endeared himself to the Tennessee people forever. This decision is a great testament to our program, that Peyton believes in what we're doing and that he looks forward to being a part of it on a continuing basis.* 99
>
> —*Tennessee head coach Phillip Fulmer*
> *March 5, 1997*

whose May 19, 1949, birthday was listed in a compilation of significant dates in Rebel football history. The Drew, Mississippi, native was a 1969–70 All-America at Ole Miss and was a legendary figure in Rebel lore. He was entering his sixth season with the Saints, in a pro career that included stops at New Orleans (1971–81), Houston (1982–83), and Minnesota (1983–84). He was third in the 1970 Heisman Trophy vote, a broken arm in the Houston game that season killing his chances. He was a 1989 inductee into the College Football Hall of Fame. His wife was an Ole Miss Homecoming Queen. Such is the stuff of which Southern football legends are made. One writer noted

Williams were listed as the team's likely all-star candidates. The Duke Blue Devils loomed on the horizon for the season opener on September 11. After a 7–5 season in 1975, no one really knew what to expect in 1976.

Phillip Fulmer, for his part, was at Wichita State, preparing for his third season with the Shockers, and was in his second season as linebackers coach. Doug Dickey was head coach at Florida. John Majors was preparing for a national championship run at Pittsburgh, complete with a Heisman Trophy candidate named Tony Dorsett. There were rumors even then that Majors would be the next Vol head coach, rumors that proved correct when Battle resigned in November and Majors came marching home for the 1977 season.

There was, however, a more significant drama taking place some 600 miles to the southwest of Knoxville in New Orleans, Louisiana, the so-called "Crescent City." It was on that March day that New Orleans Saints quarterback Archie Manning and his wife, Olivia, welcomed their second son into the fold. His name was Peyton Williams Manning and he joined older brother Cooper in the Manning household. There would be a third Manning son a few years later, this one named Eli.

Archie Manning, Elisha Archibald Manning III for the purists, was an Ole Miss legend

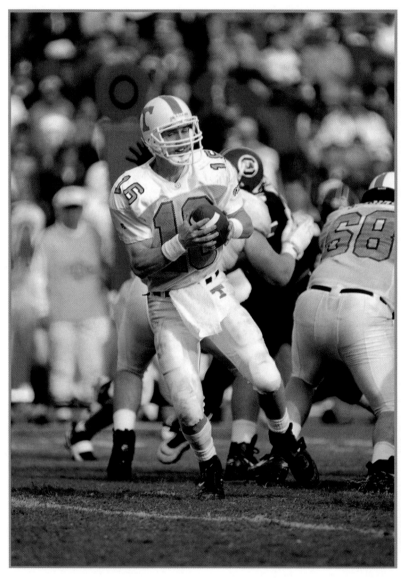

▲ *Offensive guard Spencer Riley holds out a South Carolina Gamecock as Manning drops back to pass.*

Peyton looks for the call from the sidelines as he prepares for the next play.

that characters named after Archie made appearances in two of Mississippi native John Grisham's novels, *A Time to Kill* and *The Pelican Brief.*

You could forgive Vol fans for not being excited about those events at that point in time, except for those precious few who might also have been Saints fans. After all, their last memory of Archie Manning had been seven years earlier in 1969, when a 7–0 Tennessee team headed to Jackson, Mississippi, to play an Archie Manning-led Ole Miss team. The Rebels were 5–3, but won out the rest of the season and defeated Arkansas 27–22 in the Sugar Bowl.

The final that day against the Vols was 38–0 and the Vols ended up in the Gator Bowl instead of a more likely berth in the Orange Bowl. It has been called the "Jackson Massacre." Vol fans, emboldened by a 31–0 Vol victory over the Rebels a year earlier in which Archie threw seven interceptions, wore buttons saying "Archie Who?" to the game. It was as long a day as any Vol fan has ever spent in any stadium. The perception of Archie Manning in Big Orange Country would change considerably beginning in 1994, but that's getting ahead of the story.

There's an equally compelling story, a connection that made little news at the time, but turned out to be significant. In addition to Manning, the Saints also found a place on their roster for Tennessee quarterback Bobby Scott, who had been on the opposite side of the field from Archie in

the 1968 and 1969 Ole Miss–Tennessee games. Scott was with the Saints on the active roster in 1971–72 and on the taxi squad from 1973–82. He and Manning became fast friends, watched their respective families grow up, and are friends to this day. When Archie and his family were honored by the Knoxville Area Boy Scouts, Bobby was the one who introduced them at the dinner in their honor.

As the years wore on, Peyton Manning grew and matured and by the time he was a sophomore at Isidore Newman High School in New Orleans in the 1991 season, he was ready to begin making his mark

▲ *A youthful Peyton and dad, Archie, look on intently from the sidelines.*

▲ *These are three Mannings in three different Archie jerseys: Peyton, Eli, and Cooper.*

seven TDs rushing. The team's record was 11–2 and they ended up in the state quarterfinals. He was All-Parish, All-District, Most Valuable Offensive Player, All-Metro Offensive Player, All-State Most Valuable Offensive Player, and All-South.

By the time the 1993 season rolled around, he was a pre-season Reebok All-America, on the *USA Today* Top 25 prospects list, a SuperPrep All-America, and a Blue Chip All-America. His 1993 statistics were again impressive, what with 168 completions in 264 tries for 2,706 yards

▲ *Peyton Manning seeks guidance from assistant coach Randy Sanders on the sideline.*

▲ *Archie Manning is, without a doubt, a Southern collegiate football legend, even today over 25 years after his last game.*

in gridiron circles around New Orleans and eventually across the country.

His 1991 ledger was 140 completions in 232 attempts and 2,162 yards. He had 23 TD passes against 12 interceptions. He scored three rushing TDs. The most significant stat was his team's 12–2 record and passage to the state semifinals.

In 1992, there was more of the same. He completed 144 of 264 passes for 2,345 yards. He had 30 TD passes against but four interceptions and scored

▲ *Jeff Hall knocks home an extra point in the 1996 Alabama game.*

and 39 TDs against nine interceptions. He added four rushing TDs and his team was 11–1, losing to Baton Rouge's Northeast High in the Class AA play-offs. He completed 23 of 43 passes against Zachary for 395 yards and three scores. All that translates into a 34–5 career record

▲ *Peyton compares notes with David Cutcliffe on the phone from the press box.*

▲ *Can Archie still play and do magic things with the football under his arm?*

Circle of Champions National High School Football Player of the Year and Louisiana State Player of the Year. He won the Bobby Dodd Atlanta Touchdown Club Prep Player of the Year Award.

He was a 3.3 student who scored 1050 on the SAT. He was a lower school aide, a volunteer for the Special Olympics, and a Peer Support Leader.

Recruiters came calling in droves. SuperPrep's analysis was that Peyton was the No. 3 QB in the country, behind Hines Ward of Forrest Park, Georgia, who was a Georgia signee, and Robert Reed of Brandon, Louisiana, who signed with Arkansas. The report also indicated that he was ahead of Josh Booty, who had committed to LSU.

Published reports indicated that Peyton would visit Tennessee, Michigan, and Florida, with other visits to be decided from Florida State, Notre Dame, Texas, and Ole Miss. Manning said that Vol quarterback Heath Shuler had proven helpful in the recruiting process.

"I've never been on Tennessee's campus and I want to see what it's like," Manning said in November

and 452 completions in 761 attempts. He had 92 career TDs passing.

Post-season honors came quickly. He was a member of the "Dixie Dozen," the USF&G Sugar Bowl Amateur Athlete for the month of October, and the New Orleans Quarterback Club Player of the Year. He was a Blue Chip All-America as well as a Blue Chip Academic Selection. *Parade* magazine tabbed him an All-America selection and he was Gatorade

▲ *Peyton and Cooper share a quiet moment with their dad.*

1993. "I talked to Heath about two weeks ago and he gave me a few pointers. He told me to take my visits, take good advice, and make sure you'll be happy with your decision. Heath is really a good guy, probably my favorite quarterback right now. I like the way he plays and the way he leads that team."

Back in Knoxville in the 1993 season, it was Fulmer's first full year as Vol head coach. (He had coached the first three games of the 1992 season as interim head coach, winning all three, and was named head coach just before the 1993 Hall of Fame Bowl game, a contest the Vols won over Boston College by a 38–23 count.) The 1993 Vols were led by Shuler and running back Charlie Garner and ended up 10–2 after a loss to Penn State in the 1994 Florida Citrus Bowl. (A 17–17 tie against Alabama in October had become a victory when NCAA sanctions came down against the Tide.)

But Shuler's future as a Vol was in doubt because of the lure of pro football and Heath later confirmed he was going to the pros in a January media conference, held in the same room in which Peyton announced he was staying at Tennessee just over three years later. What media conferences take away, they also give.

The recruiting season was in full swing and a few weeks later, on February 2, Fulmer and his staff landed what would become one of the best classes in the school's history. Peyton Manning was likely the top catch, along with some of the household names of Tennessee football today.

The names included linemen Jonathan Brown of Tulsa, Oklahoma, and Jeff Coleman of Gaffney, South Carolina, backs Terry Fair of Phoenix, Arizona, and Cory Gaines of Baton Rouge, Louisiana, lineman Ron Green of Severna Park, Maryland, placekicker Jeff Hall of Winchester, Tennessee, lineman Mercedes Hamilton of Waynesboro, Georgia, by way of Fork Union Military Aacdemy, backs Anthony Hampton of Englewood, New Jersey, and Steve Johnson of Powder Springs, Georgia, juco lineman Craig King of Asheville, North Carolina, via Northeastern Oklahoma A&M, backs Greg Kyler of Baltimore, Mark Levine of Dallas, Andy McCullough of Dayton, Ohio, Dustin Moore of Greeneville, Tennessee, and Marcus Nash of Tulsa, Oklahoma, linemen Will Newman of New Market (Jefferson County), Jarvis Reado of Marrero, Louisiana, and Diron Robinson of Oklahoma City, Oklahoma, and backs James Smith of Blythe, California, via Arizona Western College, Maurice Staley of Charlotte, North Carolina, and Branndon Stewart of Stephenville, Texas. It was an impressive group and Vol fans could not wait to see this group get on campus. Was this a good group or what?

Why did Peyton choose Tennessee? Here's one indication from the profile all Vol athletes fill out on their arrival on campus: *"Because I wanted to go there."*

The day he committed, a commitment to attend a certain university being a significant rite of passage, at least to the media who cover recruiting, in the recruiting wars, Peyton explained his decision as follows: *"It was a feeling I've had all along during the last two or three weeks during the visits I made and the visits with coaches that have been in my living room. Tennessee kept popping up*

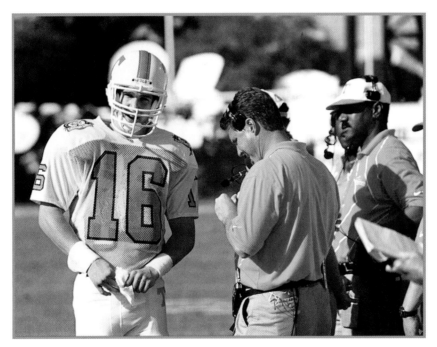

▲ *What to do now? Peyton, Randy Sanders, and the brain trust upstairs discuss their options.*

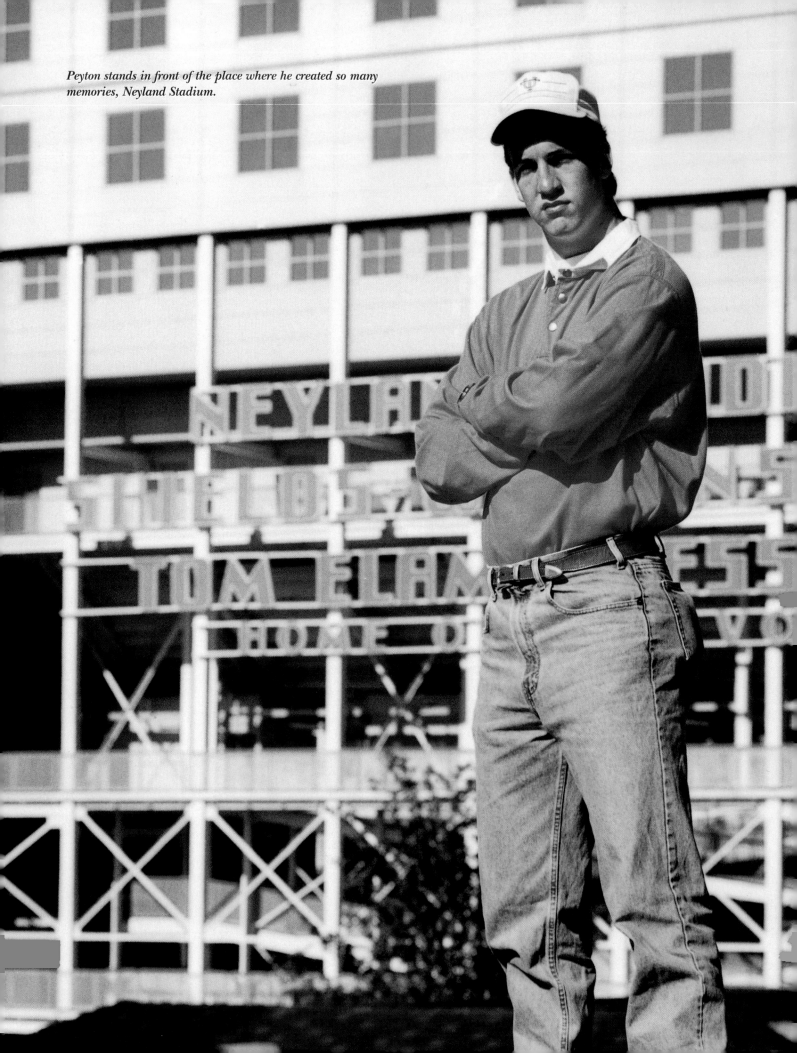

Peyton stands in front of the place where he created so many memories, Neyland Stadium.

in my head and in my heart." It was a sentiment similar to one he would express when he decided to stay at Tennessee in March 1997.

It was an agonizing time for Peyton and Archie as the recruiting process inexorably wore down. Did Peyton feel any pressure what with the name "Manning" being emblazoned on the back of whatever jersey he chose? His answer was vintage Peyton, well-thought out and reasoned. "The way I see it, being Archie Manning's son, no matter where I go it will be pressure. Being the son of a former quarterback, they expect you to do well. Going to Ole Miss will be more pressure because that's where Dad made his name."

Archie was careful to separate his role as "dad" from that of "Ole Miss alumnus," leaving the ultimate decision squarely in Peyton's lap. "I feel strongly about the fact it should be his decision," Archie said at the time. "If he wants to play football there, that's fine. If it's not the best thing for him, that's fine. I love Ole Miss but I can't say I love Ole Miss more than my son. I love him more.

"With my Ole Miss hat on, I'm disappointed like a lot of people. But with my daddy's hat on, I'm proud of the way he handled things. At 17, I couldn't have stood up to any of the stuff he has at his age."

Peyton came to campus and immediately immersed himself in learning the Vol offense. He chose No. 16 for his jersey, what with junior cornerback DeRon Jenkins already possessing the famed No. 18. He could've had No. 12, but Nash wanted it and that was that. You can't imagine Peyton asking an upperclassman or even a fellow teammate to relinquish his jersey and he didn't ask. That done, Peyton immediately threw himself to work in the film room. One journalist said "Manning watched more film

than Siskel and Ebert." He was right. Manning was also one of the last to leave the practice field each day, portraying a work ethic that many close to the Vol program consider to be legendary.

Like nearly every Vol campaign, the 1994 season was anxiously awaited and it all began in the Rose Bowl in Pasadena, California. Peyton and Branndon Stewart were on the traveling squad to UCLA as were a number of the heralded Vol frosh. With Shuler gone, the reins of the Vol attack were turned over to fifth-year senior Jerry Colquitt of nearby Oak Ridge, who had labored behind Shuler and had some impressive moments in Shuler's stead in both 1992 and 1993. It was Colquitt's time to lead the Vol offense

▲ *Peyton Manning led a late rally to subdue Vanderbilt by 12–7 in the 1995 contest at Neyland Stadium.*

▲ *Manning and Hines Ward, two of the nation's top recruits in 1993–94, share a moment after the 1997 game, a 38–13 Tennessee win.*

and no would know that his time as a starter would last but seven plays. No one would know that reserve quarterback Todd Helton, known better today with the Colorado Rockies, would quarterback the Vols until the second quarter of the Mississippi State game on October 24 and then leave with a knee injury, leaving Fulmer with rookies Manning and Branndon Stewart as his only options under center, with a 1–3 mark staring the Vols squarely in the face. Again, we get ahead of the story.

When the Vols received the opening kickoff at UCLA, moving from north to south, adversity struck within minutes. Colquitt limped off the field and would never play another down for the Vols. Helton entered the game and, with Manning and Branndon Stewart making cameo appearances (neither of which was memorable), the Bruins used a 54-yard TD pass and four field goals to take an 18–0 lead.

Helton led the Vols off the mat by throwing a TD pass to wideout Courtney Epps, and sending Mose Phillips and James Stewart (no relation to Branndon) into the end zone on short runs. Helton, definitely a determined competitor, made a key block downfield on a pass to Nilo Silvan. Joey Kent and Billy Williams caught two-point conversion passes, but the Vols lost by 25–23. Freshmen Brown, Fair, Johnson, and Hampton each saw action, joining Manning and Branndon Stewart.

When Colquitt went down, Vol Network broadcaster Bill Anderson hit the bottom of the broadcast table, bemoaning the loss of the senior signal-caller, a scene which was repeated across Big Orange Country. What was a broken dream for Colquitt became a great opportunity for Manning, although no one outside the Vol family really knew it at the time.

Manning and Branndon Stewart watched from the sidelines as the Vols dismantled Georgia a week later before 86,117 at Sanford Stadium in Athens. James Stewart scored four TDs and rushed for 211 yards and the Vols overcame a rough place or two in the second half to win by 41–23. Stewart had a 71-yard sprint down the left sideline that broke the game open as part of 383 rushing yards the team amassed on the evening. The Vols threw but 13 passes as the good guys up front dominated the proceedings all night. The Vols also did not lose a turnover. Rookie defensive back Terry Fair, for his part, led the Vols with eight tackles. It was the last time Peyton would not step onto the field for the Vols.

The next week was the home opener. After 25 years on various types of artificial surfaces, the Vols were going back to grass on the floor of Shields–Watkins Field. That was the good news. The bad news was having to play Florida. A capacity crowd of 96,656 saw the game with millions more watching on ESPN. The Gators won by 31–0, the first blanko job on the Vols in Neyland Stadium since the 1980 Alabama game when the Tide won 27–0.

Manning had a brief appearance and threw an apparent TD pass to Silvan, but saw the play called back because the rookie quarterback had broken over the line of scrimmage. Both young quarterbacks had modest stats, Manning 3-of-5 for 27 yards, Branndon Stewart 6-of-8 for 85 yards with a 30-yard run thrown in.

Things definitely hit a low point the next week as Helton banged up a knee and the Vols blew a 21–7 lead in the third quarter and lost in the final seconds by a 24–21 count. Manning's first TD pass as a Vol went 76 yards to Kendrick Jones in the first quarter and he added another to Joey Kent in the second. The Vols inexplicably lost four turnovers in the final stanza and State scored the wining TD with less than a minute to go in the game.

With Helton out, the responsibilities for running the Vol offense fell on the shoulders of Manning and Branndon Stewart. Washington State was next up and being the nation's No. 1 defensive team, the game proved to be a defensive struggle. Silvan scored the game's only TD on a 62-yard reverse and John Becksvoort's 27-yard field goal proved to be the ultimate margin of victory. Manning had a key pass to Jones for 41 yards that set up Becksvoort's boot.

Manning became the first pure frosh to start at quarterback since Alan Cockrell did likewise in the 1981 Colorado State game. The Vols unveiled a new look on defense as Ben Talley moved to defensive end, Scott Galyon moved to outside linebacker, and Tyrone Hines moved to middle linebacker. Tom Hutton maintained the field position edge for the Vols with two booming fourth-quarter punts. He averaged 46.2 on the day.

Manning showed a portent of things to come the next week against Arkansas. The Vols had a 21-point second quarter that turned the game in the right direction. Manning threw a 23-yard TD pass to Mose Phillips and a 27-yard scoring toss to James Stewart. Hines had a 38-yard fumble return for a score. Manning completed 12 of 18 passes for 157 yards.

▲ *Peyton offers his thoughts on the action on the field.*

*The Thrill of Victory!
Peyton and the famed
Beer Barrel at Kentucky!*

When Alabama came to town a week later, Manning hit 10 of 18 passes for 138 yards and Aaron Hayden rushed for 145 yards, second best mark of his career. The Vols led 13–10 before Jay Barker led a TD drive that gave the Tide the lead at 17–13.

Belying his youth, Manning led the Vols back downfield before the drive stalled at the Tide 7. In the game story in *Volunteers Magazine* the next week, it was written that, "It was a classy drive, one perhaps reminiscent of a man named Manning wearing No. 18 on his blue jersey 25 years or so ago. Manning led the Vols down the field with help from Aaron Hayden and Joey Kent and nearly pulled off the miracle comeback. It was a finish that left the multitudes breathless, but the Tide went homeward with the victory." Just for the record, as you will see, the Tide hasn't defeated the Vols since.

In one of the few games of Peyton's career that wasn't televised, the Vols took the measure of South Carolina at Williams–Brice Stadium a week later as Manning continued to sparkle under center. Peyton threw two TD passes to James Stewart and added a third to Kent. The toss to Kent came just before halftime and allowed the Vols to lead by 24–3. Tennessee's offensive front did not allow a sack and nine different receivers caught passes for the Vols. Jones found Branndon Stewart for another completion. Manning hit 18 of 23 passes for 189 yards.

The kicking game proved pivotal in a 24–13 win over Memphis two weeks later. Hayden rushed for 129 yards and Phillips scored twice. The Vols scored on short drives after field position engendered by the kicking game. Silvan had returns of 57, 15, 40 (off a reverse from Shawn Summers), and 24 yards to set up three scores and a Becksvoort fielder. Branndon Stewart led the Vols to 10 second-half points and made a nifty fake on Phillips' second TD.

It all started really coming together for the Vol offense the next two weeks, against old and venerable rivals Kentucky and Vanderbilt. The rookie signal-callers were playing with the poise of grizzled veterans.

The Vols took Kentucky by 52–0 as Manning threw TD passes to Williams and Kent, and Hayden rushed for 79 yards and scored twice. The Vols thus posted their most lopsided victory in the history of the series. Manning added a TD on a 10-yard run, his first TD run as a Vol. It was simply a day in which the Vols scored first, last, and often.

The onslaught continued the next week in Nashville against Vanderbilt, as the Vols played one of only three games on the ersatz surface during the Manning years. Manning had a 20-yard TD pass to Silvan and a 3-yarder to tight end David Horn. James Stewart became the Vols' all-time leading rusher with 121 yards on the day, 1028 on the season, and 2890 for his career.

Lance Wheaton, normally employed as a holder for Becksvoort's kicks, saw action at quarterback and Helton, injured way back in the Mississippi State game, also saw action under center.

The resurgence from 1–3 to 7–4 earned the Vols a Gator Bowl bid to play Virginia Tech and, while the Hokies had great enthusiasm before the game, the Vols put it all together to take a 45–23 decision at Florida Field. What was really eerie about the game

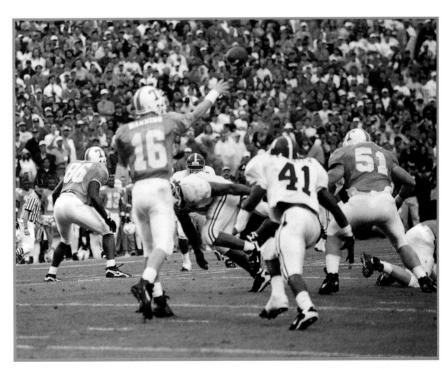

▲ *The ball has just left Peyton's hand and it looks to be another big play.*

▲ *Joey Kent (11), who caught a school-record 183 passes during his career good for 2814 yards and 25 scores, turns a reception upfield for big yardage.*

was seeing an Orange and White checkerboard, the trademark of Vol football at Neyland Stadium, in the north end zone.

The Vols led 14–0 at the quarter and 35–10 at the half. Manning threw a 36-yard TD pass to Nash and completed 12 of 19 passes for 189 yards. He added a 29-yard run. James Stewart rushed for 85 yards and three TDs and threw a TD pass to Jones covering 19 yards.

Kent made a diving catch of a Manning toss to set up the TD pass to Nash and the Vols made the most of possession time in the first half, scoring 35 points in but 11:46 game time.

Manning was named SEC Freshman of the Year and became a quarterback of national renown despite his relative youth. He had led the Vols to a 7–1 record as a starter and finished the season with 89 completions in 144 attempts for a completion percentage of .681 and 1141 yards. He had led the Vols out of the darkness, into the light.

Perhaps seeing the handwriting on the wall, Branndon Stewart left Big Orange Country during the winter, heading southward to Texas A&M.

The 1995 season was one of the most exciting in recent memory, replete with high-scoring shootouts and dog-eat-dog defensive struggles. For the offensive-minded, there were nuggets like the 41–14 conquest of Alabama, the 56–21 triumph over South Carolina, and thrillers with Kentucky and Vanderbilt in the traditional season-ending games.

In that season, Tennessee racked up a 10–1 record, finished fourth in the final regular-season national polls, and met Ohio State in the Citrus Bowl. More about that little surprise momentarily.

The Vols cranked up an 87-yard TD drive on their first possession against East Carolina and went from there to a 27–7 victory in the first gridiron meeting between the two schools. Manning was 6 for 6 and scored the first TD of the young season on a quarterback sneak. North Carolinian Jay Graham gave notice that he would be a more-than-accurate replacement for James Stewart and Hayden with 26 carries for 144 yards, first of 11 games out of that season in which he cracked the century mark. Manning had a 31-yard TD pass to Silvan.

Manning completed 17 of 29 passes for 178 yards to eight different receivers. While the first TD drive took 8:04 off the clock, Manning led two other TD drives that together were 3:47. Leonard Little, who would later serve as co-captain of the 1997 team with Peyton, had an auspicious debut, with five stops, a sack, and two tackles for loss.

Georgia proved to be a tougher test the next week, taking the first drive of the game in for a score, leading on more than one occasion and having a shot at a tie-breaking field goal in the waning moments. Manning was up to the task, however, completing 26 of 38 passes for 349 yards and two scores, one to Ronnie Pillow and the other to Kent.

Manning was at his best when the Vols got the ball back after Georgia misfired on a late field goal at the south end. The winning drive was keyed by a 29-yard screen pass from Peyton to Graham and culminated on the game winner, a 34-yarder by Hall. Pillow had the most intriguing stats of the night, with one catch for one yard and one TD.

The next week saw a big one get away. Tennessee twice led by 16 points in the first half, but fell victim to 48 unanswered Gator points in losing a 62–37 decision. The Vols had scored 30 first-half points as Manning threw two TD passes to Nash, Chester Ford scored on a short run, and Raymond Austin had a 46-yard fumble recovery for a score. Hall added a field goal.

The game got away in the second half on turnovers and some poor work in the kicking game. Manning completed 25 of 36 passes for 326 yards and made the stop on Florida's Fred Weary way downfield after a Vol fumble.

▲ *Brent Gibson (51) offers protection as Peyton decides whether to hand off to Jay Graham (25) or wing the ball downfield.*

▲ *Vol linebacker Tyrone Hines celebrates a big play!*

The Vols responded the right way the next week, taking the measure of Mississippi State by 52–14, after leading 31–0 at halftime. Manning threw a two-point pass to Jeremaine Copeland and led a Vol attack that racked up 254 yards rushing and 260 yards passing, in that offensive balance coaches always talk about on their television shows.

It was a game in which the Vols did not lose a fumble or give up a sack. Manning completed 21 of 35 passes on a cold and windy day in Knoxville. The Vols had five rushing TDs.

The next week at Knoxville, the Vols defeated Oklahoma State 31–0 with Graham rushing for 108 yards and Manning throwing TD passes to McCullough and Kent.

At Arkansas the next week, it was an offensive shootout in which the Vols came back from two 10-point deficits to win by 49–31. Down 24–14 with 6:07 to go in the second quarter, the Vols ran off a 35–7 streak that led to the eventual 18-point margin. Graham ran for 130 yards and three scores and Manning ran a potent offense that rang up 521 yards total, 384 passing. Manning completed 35 of 46 passes for his day's work and threw for four TDs, to Kent twice, Eric Lane, and Staley.

The Vols had the ball 32:07 and had 32 first downs. Kent's first TD was of the "bomb" variety down the far sideline and was part of a 13-catch day for 161 yards. Nash added seven catches for 97 yards, Staley four for 36.

The next week was Alabama at historic Legion Field in Birmingham, a stadium in which the Vols had lost in 1987, 1989, and 1991. Archie Manning had dueled Alabama's Scott Hunter on this same field in 1969 in a game in which the duo combined for 55 completions to establish a national record and 24 national, SEC, and team records fell.

Always the student of history, Peyton knew the Vols had to make something happen quickly to get momentum in the Vols' favor. How quickly? Real quickly. Like on the first play. Manning found Kent for a dramatic 80-yard score on the game's first play to put momentum squarely in the Vols' corner. The Vols led 21–0 as Peyton found Nash for a score and Manning surprised everybody by seemingly sending Graham over the top for the score, but no, not really. Manning kept the ball and scored on a bootleg left as

Vol kicker Jeff Hall and holder Jason Price celebrate a successful placement kick.

everyone, including the officials, wondered where the ball was. There it was, in Manning's mitts in the northwest corner. It was 21–0 at that point, 28–7 at the half, after another Manning TD pass to Nash.

▲ *Peyton examines the action closely from the sidelines.*

one was too good for words. It was the third time the Vols had scored 41 points on the Tide at Legion Field, the others being in 1969 and 1983, both Vol wins.

The Vols returned home to face South Carolina two weeks later and the first blow was struck by the defense. When South Carolina tried a field goal on its first possession, Little blocked it and Hines raced 90 yards for the game's first score. The Vols put 49 points on the board in the second and third quarters, as Manning threw four TD passes to Kent twice, Graham, and Scott Pfeiffer. Holder Jason Price added another on a fake field goal just before halftime.

Manning had 16 completions in 20 attempts for 215 yards. Graham rushed for 126 yards. In addition to the blocked kick, Little stopped a fourth down try by the Gamecocks.

Tennessee defeated Southern Mississippi 42–0 the next week, scoring on drives of 27, 35, 17, and 14 yards after a 63-yard drive on their first possession. Manning tossed TD passes to Moore and Kent and was 20 of 39 for 230 yards.

It was 28–14 when Manning made his second key play of the night. With the Legion Field crowd in full roar, looking for something, anything, to key a rally, Manning and the Vols had the ball first-and-10 at their 25. Graham got the ball on a sweep right and motored down the sideline in front of the Vol bench for 75 yards and a score. School was out. It was 35–14 and the finale was 41–14. The Vols had not beaten the Tide since 1985 and this

▲ *Peyton hits at center against Georgia.*

Austin blocked a punt that Mark Levine took in for a score and the Vols had 10 lost-yardage tackles.

Kent had six catches for 77 yards and Graham rushed 26 times for 108 yards.

The next two games were a little hairy. Kentucky led 24–9 in the third quarter before Manning and his receivers led the game-winning comeback. Manning threw TD passes to Kent and Kyler and Austin blocked a last-ditch Kentucky field goal. Kent's TD covered 70 yards, while the game winner to Kyler covered 15 yards.

Little had 10 tackles, two assists, four tackles for loss, and two sacks. His running mate at end, Steve White, had two tackles for losses, a pass broken up, and a caused fumble. Tennessee had the ball 25:57, but ran 78 plays. The Vols trailed for the first time since the second quarter of the Arkansas game back in October.

The Vanderbilt game the next week was a struggle all the way that was not decided until the final moments when Vol defenders rose up to stop the Commodores. The Vols trailed 7–6 well into the final quarter before Manning and the Vol offense cranked up a 69-yard drive for the winning score. The Vol offense, led by tackle Jason Layman up front, made it happen, with Graham, who had 211 yards on the day, scoring the decisive TD with 2:59 left.

Manning had begun the drive with a 21-yard pass to Nash and Graham had a 21-yard run to get it close.

▲ *Peyton and Smokey exchange pleasantries in Manning's last run through the "T" before the 1997 Vanderbilt game.*

The two teams punted 21 times and Vol defenders gave up but 112 yards after Vandy's game-opening drive for a score. There were 16 Vol seniors who played their last home game.

The win earned the Vols a berth in the Citrus Bowl against Ohio State. The 11–1 mark was the Vols' best since 1989 and fifth 11-win season in school history. The game was played in a steady rain that was downright heavy at times. It was a Big Orange day in Orange County. Ohio State had the stars, Orlando Pace, Terry Glenn, Heisman Trophy winner Eddie George, et al., but the Vols won the game.

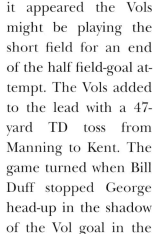

The Vols scored on their last possession of the first half as Graham broke loose for a 69-yard TD run, just when it appeared the Vols might be playing the short field for an end of the half field-goal attempt. The Vols added to the lead with a 47-yard TD toss from Manning to Kent. The game turned when Bill Duff stopped George head-up in the shadow of the Vol goal in the second quarter.

Graham ran for over 100 yards for the 11th time in 12 games. His 154 yards rushing matched a similar figure by Johnnie Jones in the 1983 contest against Maryland. The win propelled the Vols to a No. 2 finish in the CNN-*USA Today* poll and a third-place finish in the final AP poll.

Manning finished sixth in the Heisman Trophy balloting and racked up 2954 yards passing and a best-ever passing percentage (64.2%). He was named to the SEC Academic Honor Roll with a 3.49 GPA in Business Management and lifted his record as UT's starter to 18–2. He was All-SEC as selected by the Coaches, second team by AP. He was a finalist for the Davey O'Brien Quarterback Award and Football News Offensive Player of the Year.

Coming into 1996, Peyton was a pre-season All-America selection and brought a thick catalog of qualities to the Vol signal-caller position. He worked, and worked, and worked some more, because, as his position coach David Cutcliffe said, "No matter what Peyton achieves, he keeps working hard because he knows there is always room for improvement."

Neyland Stadium had been expanded at the upper north end and a crowd of 106,212 showed up for the season opener against UNLV. The Vols won by 62–3, scoring 21 first-quarter points in front of the 12th largest crowd in NCAA history. Graham and Mark Levine each scored twice and Manning threw a 63-yard TD pass to Kent. He also scored on a 1-yard run. Kent caught six passes for 151 yards and was joined cracking the century mark by Nash who caught six for 103. Fair and freshman linebacker Eric Westmoreland had fumble recoveries for scores and Copeland had a 10-yard run.

The next week saw the continuation of the historic Tennessee–UCLA series, this time on a CBS prime-time game. The Vols won 35–20, but the game had enough twists and turns to keep the 106,297 in attendance in their seats to the finish. It was another in a series of tightly contested games the Vols and Bruins had played in a series which dates to 1965.

Manning completed 16 of 28 passes for 288 yards and TDs to Eric Lane and Kent, Kent's a neatly executed hook-and-go that covered 53 yards. Manning had two 1-yard TD runs and Fair had an 86-yard punt return that was nearly perfectly executed. It came with 11:45 left and was also one of the game's pivotal moments. Kent caught seven passes for 114 yards and Nash added four for 135 in a brilliant performance. He had back-to-back 100-yard receiving games for the first time in his career.

Florida came to Knoxville two weeks later and the Vols dug themselves into a huge hole before recovering to make a game of it. On a rainy afternoon in Knoxville, Heisman Trophy winner Danny Wuerffel led the Gators to a 35–0 lead in the first 19:54 and Steve Spurrier's team had enough left in the tank to take a 35–29 win. Both Manning and Wuerffel had four TD passes, but four Gator interceptions proved pivotal. The game also proved pivotal as neither team lost a conference game thereafter.

Manning had 492 yards passing, a school record, and completed 37 of 65 passes, also school records. He threw TD passes to Peerless Price and Lane and two to McCullough. Kent and Price each went over the century mark receiving, with Price having seven catches for 161 yards and Kent having seven catches for 107 more.

The Vols went to Memphis for a Thursday night game against Ole Miss and expanded a 17–3 lead to 31–3 in the early moments of the third quarter to take a 41–3 decision. Nash had a TD pass from Manning, Lane, Graham, and Levine had TD runs, and Bill Duff scooped up a fumble and scored.

It was the Vols' second win on a Thursday night in as many tries and marked the first game against the Rebels since 1991. Little was named SEC Defensive Player of the Week for a five-tackle, three-sack, and two forced-fumble effort. It was also an emotional contest for the Manning family. Peyton, who has a good handle on these things, handed the game ball to Archie and said simply, "This is special."

Archie, in turn, said Peyton seemed focused. "Ole Miss is in for a tough game tonight because he's ready," Archie told Olivia. After the game he said, "Peyton knows his role as a quarterback and as a leader. He knows where his priorities are, and I'm proud of the way he handled the pressure tonight."

The Georgia game 10 days later saw a 29–17 Vol win and one of the most intriguing plays of the Manning era. The Vols never trailed, but needed interceptions from Raymond Austin and Terry Fair to cinch the deal. Manning showed his versatility in tossing TD passes to Kent and Nash.

He dodged the rush long enough to find Kent in the end zone for one score and, when a quarterback sneak was stuffed at the line, he had the poise to roll out, taking the Great Circle Route to his right around referee Bill Goss, and find Nash at the right corner. It was a classic play, one sure to be talked about over the years. Hall added four field goals, Hines had an interception, and Austin added a fumble recovery.

▲ *The vintage Manning passing form.*

Tide got it close on their ensuing possession, Little forced a fumble that Jonathan Brown recovered and the Vols had the win.

At Columbia a week later, the Vols were seriously challenged at 21–14 and were backed up to their goal line. The Vols did, however, make the required plays when they had to and escaped with a 31–14 win in front of a record crowd on the Fairgrounds at Williams–Brice Stadium. Manning completed 27 of 36 passes for 362 yards and two scores, one each to McCullough and Kent. Price scored on a 54-yard run as Manning sent the flow of the play one way and Peerless the other. Graham had the Vols' first score on a 6-yard run.

Little was lost for the season with a knee injury in the second half, but had seven tackles, including two for losses and 2.5 sacks, before leaving. Manning was named SEC Player of the Week for his efforts.

The next game at Memphis was one of those inexplicable contests where a favored team lets an underdog hang around and ends up paying for it. The Vols led 17–14 before the Tigers had a 69-yard drive for the game winner.

The next week, the Vols broke open a close game with 14 points in the third quarter and 27 in the fourth to take a 55-14 win over Arkansas. Terry Fair's 86-yard punt return opened the floodgates and the Vols never looked back. Troy Pratt had a key block to spring Fair on his return.

Manning completed 28 of 41 passes for 282 yards and threw two TD passes to Kent and one to Nash. Rookie defensive back Dwayne Goodrich stole the show in the fourth quarter with two fumble recoveries and an interception return for a score. Kent's TD reception came after the Vols took a field goal off the board because of a penalty.

In the home finale and last game for Kentucky coach Bill Curry, Tennessee led 14–10 after one period, but scored the next 42 points to take a 56–10 victory. Peerless Price caught TD passes of 80 and 59 yards and Jay Graham ran for scores of seven and 35 yards. Man-

Two weeks later, not on the "Third Saturday in October," but on the fourth (it still counts) Saturday, the Vols came off the mat of a 13–0 third-quarter deficit and finally escaped with a 20–13 victory, their second triumph in as many years over the Tide.

Manning found Kent for 54 yards and the good guys' first score and Graham scored after an interception by Fair got it close. Later, the Vols had it at their 21 when Graham hit the right side of the line and found the wide open spaces for a 79-yard TD run that killed the Tide's chances for a second straight year. When the

ning completed 16 of 23 passes for 317 yards and three scores, the third a 38-yarder to McCullough.

Manning passed the 3,000-yard mark for the season, first Vol to do so. Kentuckian Chester Ford added a TD as did sub quarterback Jeremaine Copeland on a nifty 30-yard run. Goodrich recovered a fumble, his fourth grab of a turnover in the past two games.

The regular season ended with a night game at Vanderbilt. Under cold, rainy skies, the Vols jumped to a 14–0 second-quarter lead, but had to battle hard to escape with a 14–7 win.

Graham, one of 19 seniors closing out their Vol careers scored the first TD, while Hines scooped up a fumble and ran 61 yards for a score. Graham's TD culminated a 12-play, 72-yard drive and came from four yards out. Austin and Fair had drive-stopping interceptions in the fourth quarter. The Vols held the Commodores to four first downs, minus-1 yards rushing, and 139 total yards in a solid defensive performance. Corey Terry had eight tackles, including three lost-yardage hits and 1.5 sacks.

In early December, Manning finished eighth in the Heisman voting.

▲ *The 1994 Vol quarterbacks with David Cutcliffe (L-R): Peyton Manning, Mike Grein, Jerry Colquitt, Todd Helton, and Branndon Stewart.*

No one knew what to expect from Big 10 co-champ Northwestern in the 1997 Citrus Bowl, but the Vols hit the purple and black, that's right, purple and black, clad Wildcats with a lethal dose of speed and quickness. The Vols jumped out 21–0 as Manning hit Price and Kent for scores and scored one himself on another bootleg on which the flow went one way and he went another.

Northwestern tied the game 21–21, thanks to some ill-timed Vol penalties and turnovers (aren't they all?), but Manning found Kent for 67 yards and a TD and led a beat-the-halftime-clock drive for a Hall fielder just before the horn.

Hines had an interception return to break the game open in the third quarter and Manning found Moore for the game's final score. As the game ended,

▲ *Peyton and fellow captain Leonard Little before the SEC Championship game.*

Vol fans chanted for Peyton Manning to stay one more year after he had dismantled the Wildcats to the tune of 27 for 39 passing for 408 yards and four scores. The Vols' overall record of 10–2 was thus accomplished by a high-scoring offense combined with a grudging defense that finished first in the SEC and among national leaders.

The big story leading into the 1997 season would happen off the field and not resolve itself until March. Manning would distinguish himself off the field and provide the answer to Vol fans' hopes and prayers in an early March media conference.

▲ *Vol cheerleaders at the Florida Citrus Bowl with plenty of Florida citrus.*

The thrill of a bowl victory: Tennessee 48, Northwestern 28.

by and said, 'Thanks.' I remember being introduced as, 'senior quarterback Peyton Manning.' That sounded good to me."

His senior year was the stuff of which dreams are made. Here's the story.

Manning and Little had been elected captains in the spring, along with alternate captains Brown, Duff, Nash, and offensive tackle-turned-center Trey Teague. There were record-setting performances along the way by both sides of the ball as the team overcame a seemingly killer loss at Florida on September 20 (with more than a little help from LSU and Georgia) to annex the school's 12th SEC title, second in the 1990s. The Vols, showing a substantial mix of grit and resiliency, reeled off nine straight victories, including a 30–29 win over Auburn in the SEC Championship game.

Manning took on heroic proportions as a brilliant passer and field general. He sparked the Vols not only to an 11–2 record his senior season, but was 39–5 in his nearly four years as Vol signal-caller. In the victory over Auburn, first game for these two ancient rivals since 1991, he became the SEC's all-time leading passer with 11,201 yards. Little split his time between linebacker and defensive end and the Vol defenders had 47 sacks, eclipsing the previous record of 42 set a year earlier.

If all the events of the previous winter and spring had any effect at all on Manning and the Vols, it was hard to tell when Tennessee opened against Texas Tech. It was a 10–3 game late in the second quarter when the Vols scored 35 unanswered points to lead 45–3 after three quarters and win going away. A crowd

His press conference on March 5 was, as we have said earlier, one of his finest hours as a Vol. Tennessee faithful in the room broke into cheers when he announced he was staying at Tennessee for his senior season.

He followed that up by graduating a year ahead of his class in May and being named Phi Beta Kappa. He won a Chancellor's Citation for Extraordinary Service to the University. Manning was second team All-SEC and All-America. He was named to the CFA Scholar–Athlete team with a 3.61 GPA in Speech Communication.

He even said he enjoyed hearing his name over the public address system as Tennessee's quarterback at the 1997 spring game. "A lot of people just stopped

Vol fans whoop it up after a big play!

▲ *Things are getting ready to happen as Peyton searches out a receiver.*

The always-pivotal game with Florida turned the Gators' way early as the Vols' arch-rivals put 14 points on the board early and, despite three TD passes by Manning, never trailed on a hot and muggy day in Gainesville.

The Vols closed the margin to 14–7 late in the half as Manning found Copeland for a score, but Florida answered with another TD seconds before halftime and the Vols could never get closer than 12. Manning threw second-half TD passes to Copeland and freshman wideout Cedrick Wilson, but showed the effects of the loss after the game.

The Vols returned home to face Ole Miss and discovered a running back, the missing ingredient in the first three games. The Vols had struggled on the ground and turned to freshman Jamal Lewis, a highly touted Atlanta native, who responded with 22 carries for 155 yards, including a 42-yarder for the game's final score. Manning added TD passes to Nash and McCullough and Goodrich, always a Johnny-on-the-spot in the secondary, had an interception return for a score.

of 106,285, fourth largest in Tennessee history, saw Manning complete 26 of 38 passes for 310 yards and five TDs. Nash caught seven for 112 yards and two scores, with Price, Copeland, and Andy McCullough grabbing the other tosses.

It was a hot day on the West Coast when Manning returned to the venue where it all began four years earlier. This time, Peyton was the starter and led the Vols to victory, fourth for the Vols in the last five tilts against the Bruins. The Vols led 24–3 at the half, 27–6 after three quarters, but had to battle hard in the final canto to garner the victory.

Manning threw TD passes to Copeland and Nash and Little forced a safety and Gaines took an interception back 57 yards for a score. The Vols could muster but two Hall field goals in the second half and needed them both desperately as things turned out. Manning completed 28 of 49 passes for 341 yards in front of another national television audience, this time on ABC.

▲ *Peyton listens intently to advice from the bench.*

Coach Fulmer and offensive tackle Jarvis Reado prepare to board the bus on the way to the game.

onslaught on Vol passing marks with 24 of 44 passing for 324 yards. Al Wilson, rapidly becoming a force at linebacker, had 12 tackles and a tackle for loss, a sack, and caused a fumble in addition to foiling a fake field goal attempt.

Georgia was next and the Vols played perhaps their best game of the season on both sides of the ball. Like Virginia Tech a few years earlier, the Bulldogs were fired up as they left the field after pre-game warmups and played the role to the hilt with their crowd, but the Vols made it happen once the game started.

Lewis, an emerging force on the ground, had 232 yards rushing, most ever by a Vol true freshman, and had four runs over 30 yards against his homestate team. Manning continued his stellar play, with 31-of-40 stats passing for 343 yards and four TDs. Nash, Cedrick Wilson, Price, and Derrick Edmonds were each the recipient of a Manning TD toss. The crowd of 106,656 was the second largest in Neyland Stadium history, seventh all-time nationally. Manning became the fifth SEC quarterback to exceed 9,000 yards passing. The Vols had a 99-yard drive for a score in the second quarter to expand the lead to 21–10. There was another significant happening that day, as Florida lost at LSU, thus cracking the door open a bit for the Vols if they could keep winning and someone else could knock off the Gators.

Then came another trip to Birmingham to play Alabama. The Vols spotted the Tide a 6–0 lead, before the very underrated fullback Shawn Bryson scored twice on runs of 19 and two yards and Manning found Copeland for TD passes of 30 and 10 yards. A 52-yard TD toss from Manning to Price in the

The Vols trailed 3–0 in the second quarter before a Nash TD pass from Manning began a 21-point blitzkreig in the final moments of the second quarter and early moments of the third quarter which put Tennessee in the driver's seat. Manning continued the

▲ *Peyton discusses a big victory with the media.*

fourth quarter was a key play in expanding the Vol lead. Manning was 23 of 37 for 304 yards, with Copeland and Nash combining for 11 catches for 147 yards.

Manning thus became the first quarterback to lead his team to three consecutive victories over Alabama. Walk-on Eric Brown blocked a punt that led to a third-quarter score for the Vols. In his career, Manning was 65 of 109 for 919 yards and seven TDs against Alabama. It was the sixth time in as many starts in 1997 that Manning had cracked the 300-yard mark.

November 1 was significant in two ways. The Vols defeated South Carolina 22–7 on a cold day in Knoxville and Georgia, the "someone else" mentioned earlier, knocked off Florida to give the Vols the lead in

the SEC East. Lewis rushed for 205 yards and Vol defenders had a school record-tying eight sacks and held the Gamecocks to 168 yards total offense. Lewis scored on runs of 1 and 65 yards, the latter the game clincher, and Hall added field goals of 36, 34, and 47 yards.

There was an ominous trend that had begun outside of Knoxville. Michigan's Charles Woodson had been creeping up in the Heisman polls after a strong performance against Penn State. In the weeks to come, Vol fans would become more concerned about Woodson's chances of overtaking Manning for the 1997 Heisman. Woodson was the first candidate to draw serious attention other than Manning.

But there was also more football to be played. A 44–20 victory over Southern Mississippi followed as the

▲ *Peyton gives the ball to tailback Jamal Lewis.*

into a 30–22 victory. It was a game the Vols simply refused to lose. Manning had 264 yards passing on 20 for 35 stats and found Nash for TDs covering 13 and 49 yards. Nash had five catches for 126 yards. Lewis added a 23-yard TD reception from Manning and scored the Vols' final TD.

Eric Brown had another blocked punt that led to a score. Manning became the 12th quarterback to pass the 10,000-yard mark for his career.

The Kentucky game at Lexington a week later was an offensive shootout as the Vols left Commonwealth Stadium with a 59–31 win. Manning had a 25-for-35 day passing for 523 yards and five scores, but actually fell back, if you can believe that, in the Heisman polling, as Woodson, coming with a rush, had an interception to quell an Ohio State drive, caught a 38-yard pass to set up a score, and broke the game open with a 78-yard punt return. Vol fans were beginning to worry more and more about the Heisman.

Vols, trailing 13–6 in the second quarter, scored 35 of the game's next 42 points to post a victory on Homecoming afternoon (and evening). Manning was named SEC Player of the Week for his efforts, connecting on 35 of 53 passes for 399 yards and four scores. Copeland caught 11 passes for 137 yards and a score, Nash 10 for 110 yards and two scores, and Price six for 61 yards and another score. Lewis rushed 17 times for 68 yards.

After the victory over Southern Miss, it was back to the SEC for a three-game gauntlet against Arkansas, Kentucky, and Vanderbilt. It was a tough run, but the Vols were up to the task of sweeping the trifecta and annexing the SEC crown.

It all began on a cold night in Little Rock at War Memorial Stadium. Tennessee scored the final 13 points of the game to turn a 22–17 deficit

▲ *Peyton, with fellow frosh Branndon Stewart.*

▲ *Always the leader in the huddle, Peyton gets the play called.*

Manning had three TD passes to Nash, and two others to Lewis and McCullough. Lewis had 105 yards receiving and 128 yards and three TDs rushing. The Vols averaged 10.7 yards per play, setting a school record.

If the Kentucky game was an offensive shootout, the season finale against Vanderbilt was marked by cries of "defense, defense." Vanderbilt scored first and last, but Tennessee had enough arrows in its quiver to take a 17–10 victory. Manning and his fellow seniors, 28 in all, were honored before the game and delivered the SEC crown back where it belonged, but not without a few anxious moments.

Vanderbilt led 3–0 before Manning found Copeland on a slant pattern for a 33-yard score in the second quarter at the south end. Manning ran one of his patented bootleg plays in the third quarter to expand the margin to 17–3. Lewis continued his impres-

sive running with 36 carries for 196 yards. Manning's TD run was a near carbon copy of similar runs against Alabama in 1995 and Northwestern in the 1997 Citrus Bowl.

Goodrich had two interceptions and a fumble recovery, ranging far and wide across Shields–Watkins Field to disrupt the Vanderbilt offense.

The Vols thus won the SEC East and had a date with Auburn the next Saturday night in Atlanta to determine the overall SEC winner. The Vols scored first, but the Tigers led 20–10 at the half and 27–17 in the third quarter before the Vols rallied for the narrow win.

The game-winner came on Manning's 73-yard pass to Nash with 11:41 left, culminating a night in which Manning completed 25 of 43 passes for 373 yards and four TDs. He added two TD tosses to Price and one to Copeland. Lewis had 31 carries for 127 yards.

It was the Vols' third league title in 10 years and 12th overall. The win netted the Vols a shot at Nebraska in the Orange Bowl on January 2, but there was off-the-field business for Manning to attend to in the interim.

Vol fans were probably shocked to hear of a knee injury Manning had suffered in the SEC Championship Game. It was something called a ruptured bursa sack and his knee was the size of an adult grapefruit when he went to New York for "The David Letterman Show" and the annual awards dinner for the National Football Foundation and College Football Hall of Fame.

The Letterman Show was on a Monday night and Manning seemed to enjoy the whole experience tremendously. He exchanged one-liners with Letter-man, prompting the host to say, "The kid has writers." He met country singer Shania Twain and actress Courtney Cox, and that was a treat, and was a sought-after autograph from not only Letterman staffers, but also New Yorkers in the street after the show's taping.

Manning won the Draddy Award the next night at the Waldorf-Astoria, climaxing a day in which he won the Division 1-A Scholar–Athlete Award as well as the overall Scholar–Athlete Award. It was an impressive showing for young Manning, who impressed everyone he met with the way he handled the whole deal. The Draddy Award, officially presented at the Orange & White Game in April, brought UT $135,000 and Peyton $18,000 for post-graduate study. As we will find out in a moment, it led to the creation of the Peyton Manning Scholarship.

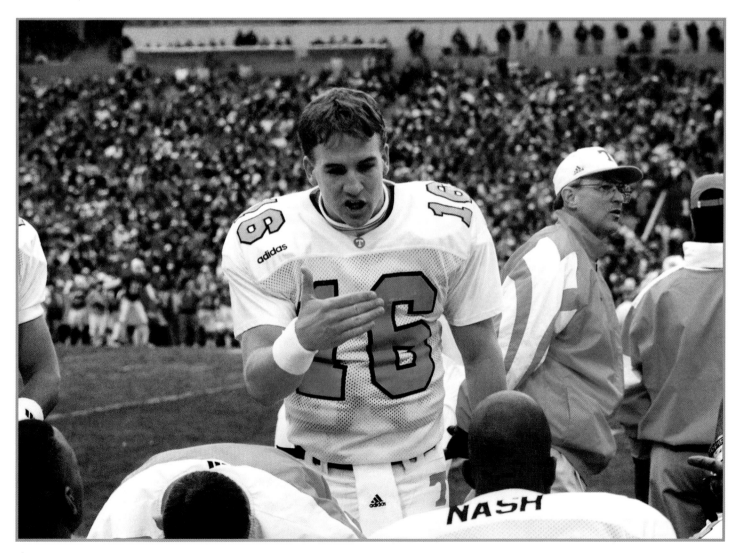

▲ *Peyton exhorts his teammates on the sideline at Kentucky.*

Manning lets it fly downfield.

Four days later, it was time for the Heisman Awards ceremonies, back in New York. In a dizzying few days, Peyton had been to Orlando for the Home Depot Awards Show, when he was named winner of the Maxwell Award as the nation's finest player, the Davey O'Brien Award as the top quarterback, and the Honda Scholar–Athlete Award. The night before the Heisman show on ESPN, he had been in Louisville accepting the Johnny Unitas Golden Arm Award.

The Heisman Show was on Saturday night, also on ESPN. The announcement came shortly after 8 p.m. and Woodson, as many in Big Orange Country had feared, got the call. It was a devastating moment.

It was, however, indicative of Peyton's character that he was the first to congratulate Woodson. If you knew Peyton, you wouldn't have expected anything less. The Heisman Awards Show was the culmination of a week in which Manning had done the University of Tennessee proud. Manning, for his part, said he felt bad for the fans, felt he had let them down. The announcement caused a stir among Tennessee fans and kept the lines on the talk shows hopping.

"I'd be less than honest if I said I didn't want to win the Heisman for the people back home in Tennessee," Peyton said. "In a lot of ways, I wanted to win it for them because they've been so supportive throughout my four years. I apologize to them. I wouldn't change a thing about this past year, or anything in my career. I wouldn't change one single thing. I did the best I could all year long and that's all I wanted to do."

The surprising turn of events put Peyton in some good company, with three other Vol legends. Vol tailback Hank Lauricella helped lead the Vols to the national championship in 1951, yet finished second to

▲ *A wave to the crowd from Peyton Manning Pass, on his way to a Vol game at Neyland Stadium.*

Princeton's Dick Kazmaier. John Majors led the Vols to a 10–0 regular season record in 1956, yet finished second to Notre Dame's Paul Hornung, who played on a 2–8 team. Heath Shuler finished second to Charley Ward of Florida State in 1993 as Ward led the parade nearly from wire to wire.

So why didn't he win? Here are some perspectives from both sides.

▲ *Peyton enjoys the victory with members of the Tennessee media.*

just that Woodson has been so spectacular that it's hard to deny him at this point."

It's a no-brainer, wrote John Borton of *Wolverine Watch,* an independent newspaper covering UM athletics. In a short essay entitled "Not By The Numbers Award," Borton wrote as follows: "Woodson's Heisman Trophy victory over statistically corpulent Tennessee quarterback Peyton Manning caused the biggest

"From start to finish, and under all that pressure of being the favorite, Peyton Manning had consistently incredible performances every week," wrote Tom Batzold of the Rochester, New York *Chronicle.* "Even though this is supposed to be a one-year award, you have to give him credit for his overall career. And him coming back for his senior season. He is a role model. He represents everything good about college football."

Conversely, there was the impact of two Woodson performances against Penn State and Ohio State. "I think quite a few Pennsylvania voters went for Woodson based on his showing against Penn State and Ohio State," wrote Ronnie Christ of the Harrisburg, Pennsylvania *Patriot.* "They were the two critical games. That's what the Heisman is all about. It's not 10,000 passing yards. It's the player who does the most for his team. Michigan is unbeaten and No. 1."

"When you watch Woodson on TV, he simply jumps out of the screen at you. It's hard to remember a player who plays primarily defense who's had as much of an impact on a top-ranked team," wrote Randy Holtz of the *Rocky Mountain News.* "I was a Manning guy until about a month ago, and I don't think that Manning has fallen down in my mind, it's

▲ *Peyton explains the basics of quarterbacking to some young athletes.*

▲ *Leonard Little makes his final run through the "T" before the 1997 Vanderbilt game.*

▲ *Peyton explains what he wants to Vol wide receivers.*

No one wanted it to end the way it did, but the memories of Peyton Manning are many and varied. It was time to put the memory banks into overdrive, to see what Peyton meant to all of us here at UT and wherever college football fans gather.

You have to give credit to Archie and Olivia, to his school teachers and coaches, and to Fulmer and his staff for the way this has all come about. There's no doubt Peyton has made us

howl in the Volunteer State since the FDA's identification of grits as hazardous waste. For once in the history of the Heisman, voters set aside their calculators, looked at overall impact, and picked the best player in the land."

With the awards out of the way, it was time for the Orange Bowl game against Nebraska. Husker coach Tom Osborne did the Vols no favor when he announced he was retiring after a distinguished career after the bowl game. It's hard enough to beat Nebraska anyway and Nebraska players had some extra incentive against the Vols.

When Michigan defeated Washington State on New Year's Day, they garnered the AP national championship. All that was left was to see if somehow Nebraska could earn the CNN/*USA Today* No. 1 team honor.

Manning's status was up in the air during pregame preparations, but you knew, in your heart of hearts, he'd play if he possibly could. He played and threw a TD pass, but the curtain rang down on his career with a 42–17 defeat. Manning threw his final TD pass to Price in the third quarter and Tee Martin gave Vol fans a glimpse of 1998 with a late drive that narrowed the margin.

▲ *The 1997 Tennessee co-captains, Peyton Manning and Leonard Little, with head coach Phillip Fulmer.*

Manning directs the band after the Vols won the 1997 SEC Championship game over Auburn.

▲ *Manning gets the opinion of the coaches in the press box about what's going on on the field.*

"Having said that the comparison is impossible and the distinction between players is slim, this newspaper would like to be on record that the 1997 Heisman Trophy, without question, belongs to Peyton Manning.

"OK, that opinion could be slightly biased. But what other college football player was forced early in his college career to start as quarterback after a teammate's injury? What other college football player makes the time and the effort to call up other young athletes in other states and in other sports to offer encouragement and friendship? What other college football player has demonstrated such remarkable leadership and consistent grace under adversity? What other college football player has been active in charity and civic efforts in his college town?

"And what other college football player—who already has a degree in hand—decided to forgo millions of dollars in a professional football contract to stay in college and play another year, just because he loves the game?

"Yes, the Heisman is supposed to go to the best football player, not the most altruistic one. But in our objective view, Manning is both.

"This year, the Heisman should go to a superb athlete, who also happens to exemplify all that is good about college athletics. We're pulling for Manning. But whether or not he wins the trophy, he should know how very proud people across Tennessee are of him."

That same day, Malcolm Moran of the *New York Times* wrote a story entitled "Manning Returned for Magic Moments, Not the Heisman Hopes." You want the real Peyton Manning, the real story about why he came back, why he wanted to be a senior. It may seem a bit old-fashioned, but here it is, a testament to Peyton Manning: *I've always been envious of those guys, as a sophomore and junior, when they were playing their last few games. You picture what they're going through. You can just see the emotion, how special their careers have been to them. I remem-*

all proud and has been a credit to the University of Tennessee.

"The Heisman Trophy, like many other awards in other fields, attempts the impossible—the selection of the best college football player in a single year," *The Tennessean,* Nashville's morning newspaper, editorialized on December 12, the day before the Heisman announcement.

"How can anyone compare a quarterback from, let's say, the Southeastern Conference to a cornerback or receiver from another conference? The positions require vastly different skills. Statistics help, but only to a point. Many of those statistics after all, reflect on the quality of a player's teammates.

"Essentially, the sportswriters and former Heisman winners who cast their votes for the Heisman are forced to make an arbitrary distinction—perhaps influenced by hype or politics—between the very top of the top-tier college football players in the land, all of whom have exceptional abilities.

▲ *Vol fans say "Thanks for the Memories" after the 1997 Vanderbilt game.*

ber even when I was thinking about leaving, I was thinking, *'It's got to be special to be a senior. You're the leaders. You've been through so much. I think everything moves so slowly. You appreciate the little things more. In freshman, sophomore, and junior years, you're just passing through. The traveling part can get a little tiring, but the destination is worth it.*"

For Peyton Manning, the journey and the destination were worth it. The young man from New Orleans has done quite well for himself. There were victories on the field, to be sure, but the greater triumph is the way it all came about, the way Peyton represented himself, his family, his team, and his university.

Manning Family Album

An early shot of the Manning family.

Always determined, regardless of the sport, Peyton heads downcourt with the ball.

Two young Mannings, apparently on their way to church.

A session on the dance floor for Peyton.

Your favorite ghost, AKA Peyton.

Cooper and Peyton with some "good-bye-cake."

Archie and Peyton in the back yard.

Peyton and friend with birthday cupcakes.

A pensive look from Peyton.

Peyton was also a factor when he had a baseball in his hand.

Peyton drives the lane leaving a defender behind him.

Peyton looks over a big-league spread of food.

Two potential baseball stars.

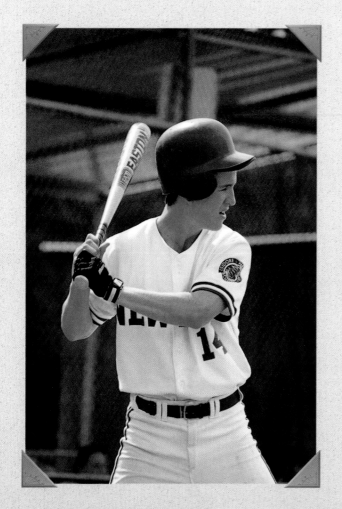

Was this guy an athlete or what?

A reflective moment for Peyton.

The old and the new, as (L-R) Jeff Staubach, Roger's son, Cooper and Peyton share a moment with the legendary pro quarterback, Sonny Jurgensen.

The thrill of victory for the Mannings after the 1995 Alabama game.

Peyton and long-time friend Randy Livingston at a school dance, complete with tux.

An unorthodox shot in a backyard game.

Peyton and Archie catch a few winks.

Peyton on the lake.

Peyton and Olivia after a game at Neyland Stadium.

*A friendly moment with
Archie and Roger Staubach.*

Some friendly
banter in the locker
room.

Perhaps mixing his sports, Peyton
discusses what to do with Archie.

Peyton and Trey Teague looking like the "Blues Brothers."

Peyton with Jim Plunkett and long-time friend Walker Jones, who played at Ole Miss.

With Knoxville Mayor Victor Ashe at the naming of Peyton Manning Pass.

More mixed sports metaphors, but the form is still good.

Peyton in the surf.

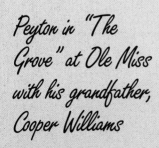

Peyton in "The Grove" at Ole Miss with his grandfather, Cooper Williams

Another scuba shot in the surf.

Peyton with Bob Griese, Roger Staubach, and Archie.

Archie with three determined-looking Manning sons.

Peyton and friends from the Class of 1997.

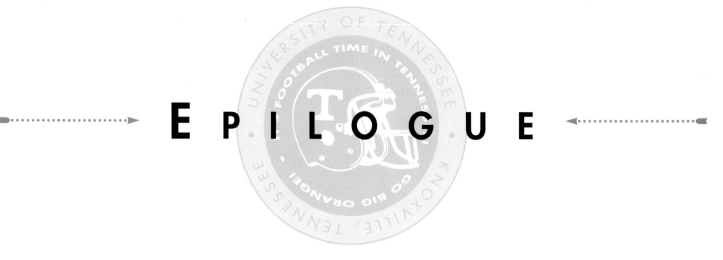

EPILOGUE

EPILOGUE: THE SEASONS OF PEYTON MANNING'S LIFE CHANGE

The seasons of Peyton Manning's life changed on April 18, 1998. The day effectively marked the end of his UT career and the beginning of his pro career. It was, as Athletic Director Doug Dickey remarked, Peyton Manning's day, summing up a collection of days which have marked the young Manning as a true Tennessee treasure.

Shortly after noon that Saturday, the Indianapolis Colts, a proud NFL franchise which had fallen on hard times in recent years, made Peyton their No. 1 draft choice, No. 1 pick overall. The pick was announced by NFL commissioner Paul Tagliabue as a

To everything there is a season, and a time to every purpose under the heaven:

A time to be born, and a time to die; a time to plant, and a time to pluck up that which is planted;

A time to kill, and a time to heal; a time to break down, and a time to build up;

A time to weep, and a time to laugh; a time to mourn, and a time to dance;

A time to cast away stones, and a time to gather stones together; a time to embrace, and a time to refrain from embracing;

A time to get, and a time to lose; a time to keep, and a time to cast away;

A time to rend, and a time to sew; a time to keep silence, and a time to speak;

A time to love, and a time to hate; a time of war, and a time of peace.

—Ecclesiastes 3: 1–8

An intent Peyton Manning thinks about the next step in his career plans.

▲ *Peyton Manning lets it fly against South Carolina.*

nation-wide audience on ESPN watched. Over 300 Vol fans who had gathered for the annual Awards Banquet of the East Tennessee Chapter of the National Football Foundation and Hall of Fame cheered when they heard the news. Even a chorus of hecklers in the New York City audience could not drown out Peyton Manning's moment, Peyton Manning's time in the spotlight.

For Tennessee fans, it was a moment of pride, a moment to look ahead and look back at the same time. The Vols had had only one prior No. 1 draft choice, 58 years earlier in 1940, when tailback George "Bad News" Cafego was the first pick of the Chicago Cardinals.

Thirty years earlier in 1968, Vol center Bob Johnson, who had been a Peyton-type figure during his career on campus (1965–67), had been the No. 1 pick of the fledgling Cincinnati Bengals en route to a distinguished career with the team from the Queen City. In

1991, the Vols had had three No. 1 picks in the draft, tackles Antone Davis and Charles McRae and wideout Alvin Harper. They duplicated that feat this season as Terry Fair (No. 20, Detroit) and Marcus Nash (No. 30, Denver), both recruits from Manning's class, also grabbed the No. 1 brass ring. So for Peyton, for Tennessee, it was quite a day.

During his career, Peyton was visible, accessible, and someone who was always there when he was needed. He was poised and polished under center and likewise made a good impression in the community. When he was in New York for the Draddy ceremonies, his fellow scholar–athletes made a beeline to him, each wanting their picture taken with him. What's more, the adults in the room did likewise. He was a modern-day Jack Armstrong, someone who made a positive impression on everyone who met him. He was a "Pied-Piper" of sorts. Lady Vol hoops star Chamique Holdsclaw, who has attained legendary status in Knoxville by leading

◀ *Now wearing the famous No. 18, Peyton Manning looks for a Colt receiver instead of one in a Tennessee uniform.*

Pat Summitt's team to three national championships, told friends she now understood what Peyton went through every time he went out.

"He's probably one of the best role models we have for our kids today," Roy Exum of the *Chattanooga Free-Press* said. "There ain't but one Peyton Manning."

April 18 was a day that saw Peyton appear at the draft with a blue No. 18 Indianapolis Colts jersey in hand, emblazoned with "Manning" on the back. For the historians in the audience, it had to have engendered some sense of déjà vú, what with that being Archie's number at Ole Miss and Peyton's high school jersey back at Isidore Newman High School in New Orleans.

▲ *Peyton prepares for mini-camp drills with the Indianapolis Colts.*

▲ *Peyton lets the offense know what's happening in the 1995 season opener against East Carolina.*

"No. 18 has always been special to our family," Peyton said. "The Colts had it available and I'm looking forward to wearing it."

It was also a day that saw Manning's No. 16 Tennessee jersey retired and presented to him in a touching ceremony later that night. That's yet to come in a day of significant transitions.

The draft ceremonies in New York were followed by a quick flight to Indianapolis, followed by an equally short jaunt to Knoxville for the spring game that evening. Things were quiet at the game, as spring games generally go, until just before halftime when Manning and his family were spotted at the northwest corner of Shields–Watkins Field. The applause spread quickly across the giant stadium where Manning had had so many of his greatest moments. It was the basic reverential type applause that turned into cheering worthy of a Saturday afternoon contest against Alabama or Florida.

If Peyton's desire in staying at UT for his senior season and spurning the blandishments of the pros was to "create more memories," he was certainly successful. With his parents, Archie and Olivia, and brother Cooper, he made his way to the stage as the theme from the movie "Superman" hit the loudspeaker, followed by that staple of Vol fans everywhere, Felice and Boudleaux Bryant's "Rocky Top."

Andy McCullough had two TD catches in the 1996 Florida game.

The honors came quickly. UT president Joe Johnson, UT Knoxville Campus Chancellor Dr. Bill Snyder, and Vice-Chancellor, Academic Affairs, Dr. John Peters, accepted a check for $135,000 from Burger King representatives Don Gleason, Russ Seuss, and Duane Setzer for Peyton's being named the Vincent dePaul Draddy National Scholar–Athlete of the Year by the National Football Foundation and Hall of Fame. Peyton also received an $18,000 post-graduate scholarship for continuation of his academic career and a specially engraved Tiffany Crystal Bowl honoring his selection. (Two of the first individual donors to the Peyton fund were Knoxvillian Herbert L. Brown and his wife, Jean, who said, simply, "they wanted to do something for Peyton" and handed a UT staffer a check for $10,000.)

The family joined Dr. Snyder and Dr. Peters in greeting the first Peyton Manning Scholarship winner, Jay Steven Burns of Bulls Gap, Tennessee, an honors graduate of Greeneville High School. He is the son of Steve and Glennis Burns. He missed his high school prom to be at the ceremonies. His résumé, like Peyton's, was pretty impressive.

He was an honor student and senior class vice president at Greeneville High School. The new academic scholarship, a four-year award covering fees and room and board at UT, honored the influence of the former Vol quarterback. Burns earned a 4.27 GPA and is the No. 1 graduate out of 197 in his graduating class.

"This is a premiere scholarship for a young man who could take his pick from among the nation's top colleges and universities," Johnson said. "He and Peyton Manning have much in common. They are strong students, athletes, and they use their gifts to help others."

Burns' volunteer activities include Habitat for Humanity, Junior Red Cross, Greene County Ministries, Holston Home for Children, and Sojourner Neighborhood Center in Washington, D.C.

Dr. Tom Broadhead, director of the UT-Knoxville honors program and member of the Manning Scholarship selection committee, said Burns, 18, was an outstanding applicant.

"Jay is a credit to his family and to Greeneville High School," Dr. Broadhead said. "He's a fine student, personable and articulate, as strong in person as he is on paper."

▲ *Peyton gets on the bus to the game.*

At Greeneville High, Burns' senior honors and activities include being named a National Merit Scholarship semi-finalist; U.S. Senate Youth Program, Tennessee's first alternate; Toyota Community Scholars; Student Council; National Honor Society; Science Club, president; Spanish Club, treasurer; Math Club, treasurer; and Scholars' Bowl, captain. Burns was second-team All-Conference in football and captain of the baseball team. The Manning scholarship is funded from gifts to the university garnered from Manning's athletic awards, the UT Athletics Department's corporate matching grants program, and other private gifts.

It is interesting to note that when a UT staffer called the Burns family about the award ceremonies, Glennis was straight to the point. After expressing her thanks for the award, she asked simply: *"Will we get to meet Peyton?"*

Following the scholarship ceremonies, Peyton then autographed a Tennessee No. 16 jersey for posterity, signing on the back just to right of his name: *"Peyton Manning, April 18, 1998."* The jersey will occupy a place of honor in the Tennessee Football Hall of Fame Exhibit in the Neyland–Thompson Center on campus. With that, he was presented a framed No. 16 jersey.

"The retired jersey will be the centerpiece of the Tennessee Football Hall of Fame Exhibit," Dickey said, "but we want to make sure that Peyton's many accomplishments are recognized. His career is one of historic proportions, involving such outstanding honors as the Sullivan, Maxwell, Davey O'Brien, and Johnny Unitas Awards. His was a unique career for the University, something we want Vol fans to enjoy in memory for all time. The Orange and White game was an opportunity for Vol fans to express to Peyton their great appreciation for how much he has done for the University."

As might have been expected, he told the appreciative crowd that he would never forget his Tennessee tenure. "I know there are people all over the country who don't realize why I'm standing here on the night I realized my dream of going to the NFL," Manning said. "It's because they have never been in this great place. It's certainly a day I'll never forget."

There was one final note. UT officials presented the 1997 SEC championship rings to Bill Duff and Chris Hogue on behalf of the team on the field and gave them to other team members after the game.

▲ *Fellow recruit Terry Fair nearly grabs an interception against Georgia.*

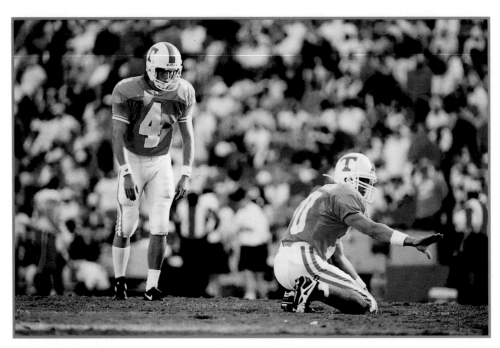

▲ *Vol placekicker Jeff Hall lines up another field goal.*

"When Peyton saw the rings, his eyes lit up and he had a big smile on his face," *Volunteers Magazine* staffer Donnell Field said. "Coach Gary Wyant gave him his ring and you could tell Peyton was impressed. There was no doubt it was a magic moment for him."

It was a magic moment in a career filled with magic moments. From his first appearance in a Tennessee game at UCLA in a white jersey, to his first TD pass as a Vol against Mississippi State, to his first win as a starter, to the pulsating rally he led in the final moments of the 1994 Alabama game (after which former Tide quarterback Scott Hunter said, "My, my, this kid is going to be a good one"), to the first play of the 1995 Alabama game (Manning to Joey Kent for 80 yards and a TD on the game's first play), to a miracle TD pass to Marcus Nash in the 1996 Georgia game, to another victory over Alabama in 1996 at Legion Field (three in all over Tide in as

many years), to his memorable announcement that he would return for his senior season. Particularly his announcement that he would return in 1997.

It remained for the Knoxville *News-Sentinel* to editorially write finis on Peyton Manning's career, when it editorialized as follows: **"Top pick a reward: Manning goes first in NFL draft and sets example as a student–athlete."**

"College football has endowed the vocabulary of sports with such terms as 'true freshman' and 'fifth-year senior.' It would be delusional to think that Peyton Manning might add another, 'master's candidate.'

"Manning, thanks to summer school and hard work, graduated cum laude from the University of Tennessee in May 1997. He would have been wealthy a year sooner if he had turned pro, but he elected to

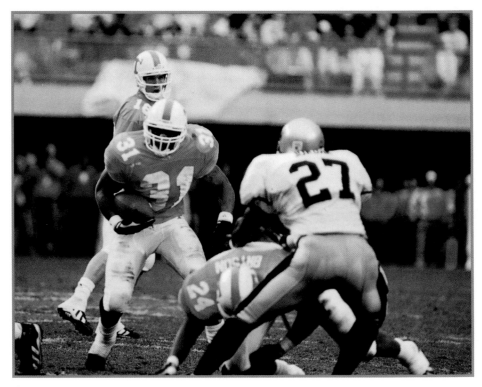

▲ *Jamal Lewis looks for yardage against Vanderbilt.*

▲ *A thoughtful moment for Peyton during a lull in the action.*

come back for his fourth and final year of eligibility as a college football player.

"Manning's decision was perhaps the most noteworthy of any UT or collegiate football player, but it was not without precedent here. Wide receiver Joey Kent, now with the Oilers, elected to stay at UT for his senior season in 1996; Peerless Price and Al Wilson chose to return for 1998.

"Nevertheless, such decisions are a departure from current practice where top athletes view college as a three-, two-, or even one-year tryout for the pros. The idea is not so much to get an education as to establish a market value.

"Manning had a different slant on the marketplace. 'You can't buy back a senior year,' he said. His return was a success but not a total fairy tale: UT did not win a national championship but did win the Southeastern Conference; he did not win the Heisman Trophy but finished second and garnered numerous other awards.

"This past weekend, he was rewarded; the No. 1 pick in the draft, with a good contract from the Indianapolis Colts to follow. With his new team, he will wear No. 18, the number his father wore at Ole Miss. Peyton Manning's jersey No. 16 was retired Saturday night in Knoxville during halftime ceremonies of the Orange and White intrasquad game.

"Manning says he plans to produce and be an asset for the Colts. 'Holdout' does not seem to be in this communications major's vocabulary.

"It would be nice to think that other athletes might follow his example."

When you think about it, you could do worse than follow the example of Peyton Manning. They say if something's "too good to be true, it ain't." Peyton Manning is the exception to that rule. He's all that's advertised. And more.

❖   ❖   ❖

Neyland Stadium is quiet now. As you walk through the south gate to the field, through the tunnel the visiting teams walk through, you get a sense of what has transpired on that famed greensward over the years. (The late Jim Satterfield, head coach at Trousdale County High School in Hartsville, Tennessee, used to sit in his office and point out the locales of the big plays on John Kerr Field just outside his window.) If you're lucky, you can walk each sideline and each end zone and remember where all the big plays happened, doing it all in the quiet of an April afternoon.

You can look across the grass-covered expanse of Shields–Watkins Field and see the football moments of your life flash in front of your eyes. In your mind's eye, you can see the great plays of Vol football transpire right there. It's the joy of being a Vol fan, or, in general, a fan of college football.

For Tennessee fans, the accomplishments of Peyton Manning on the gridiron and across the broadly defined local community will not soon be forgotten. There were times he made it look easy, but we all know it wasn't. It was the result of preparation meeting opportunity, the result of his dedication to his craft. He was something special, someone who deserves the best in whatever he does.

Vol fans were understandably disappointed in Peyton not winning the Heisman Trophy. Tennessee football is an important part of their lives and they take their heroes seriously. The temporary setbacks of life are just that, temporary impediments to bigger and better things in the days, weeks, and years to come.

Archie and Olivia's second son brought great moments to us all, moments we'll never forget.

"The thing I'll remember about Peyton," Archie said, "is how inquisitive he was. When we went on car trips, he was always asking about who I played with, what it was like to play at Georgia and LSU. He's a historian of SEC football."

He's also a young man of his word. "It was never the Jets or Tennessee," Peyton said about his decision to stay at UT. "Even if the Jets had told me they were taking me, I doubt I would have come out. I just wanted to be a senior. It was a year in college no amount of money could buy back."

It is a part of the way things work that Vol fans are looking now at Tee Martin as the Vol signal-caller in 1998. But they'll never forget the kid who came to Tennessee from New Orleans in 1994 and gave the Vols many of their finest moments. He was a captain and a leader and is now a part of the Vol legend.

To this author, Orange jersey No. 57 will always be Steve Kiner. No. 64 will always be Jack Reynolds. No. 50 will always be Chip Kell. No. 54 Bob Johnson. There's one for nearly every number.

No. 16 will always be Peyton Manning.

—Knoxville, Tennessee
May 1998

AFTERWORD

ANOTHER LOOK BACK AT TENNESSEE FOOTBALL AND PEYTON MANNING

One of the great things about college football, aspects which have been tried but not yet duplicated in the professional ranks, is the tradition each school has, magnified, if that is the proper word, by the emotional investment its fans have in their team. It's ancient and creaking stadia, the echoes of Bob Neyland at Tennessee, Bear Bryant at Alabama, Knute Rockne at Notre Dame, and Fielding "Hurry-Up" Yost at Michigan, among others, the spit-and-polish of collegiate bands (with an exception or two here and there, mostly out west) and the antics of the fans who do whatever it takes to get to the games. It's a happening. It's a unifying experience. It's memories for the ages.

"College football has meant a great deal to me," Peyton Manning has said, "and it will mean more to me the longer I live. I had a chance to pass up my senior year last year, and the more I thought about it I just thought, 'now why would you do that, to pass up this great opportunity to play this great game.' There's nothing like a Saturday afternoon on a college campus, and that's why I came back."

"For many kids, college football is a means to an end," offensive coordinator David Cutcliffe said. "Peyton has a true love of college football. He knows the way Saturdays are supposed to smell in the South."

Peyton should know. *Sports Illustrated*'s Tim Layden wrote that "Peyton immersed himself in his father's legacy after an Ole Miss fan sent the Mannings audiotapes of the Rebels' epic 1969 upsets of Georgia and LSU." (There was no mention of whether Peyton has heard the tape of the 1969 Ole Miss–Tennessee game, perhaps THE epic upset of that season.)

The story goes on to say that, "Peyton, then a junior in high school, popped the tapes into his stereo, lay across his bed and let history wash over him. He listened as his dad's offense, every member a Mississippian, was described by the play-by-play man: *'Manning brings 'em to the line. There's Mitchell from Columbus, Coker from Clarksdale . . . Manning sprints right, throws . . . touchdown! Touchdown, Ole Miss.'* Peyton memorized the calls

> **❝**People have asked me about all the attention I have received since I was in high school. It's just always been my nature to accept things, but it has really never bothered me. I have always been proud to have been Archie Manning's son. I get asked a lot if I ever get tired of being compared to him or that every article says I am the son of the former Ole Miss and Saints quarterback. But I am proud to be his son. It's never bothered me.**❞**
>
> — *Peyton Manning*
> *December 24, 1997*

> **❝** *As I have continued to work football games through the years, the colleges and the pros, the players have come on in a steady stream, always bigger, stronger, faster. And that has given us a better game than ever. Greatness must always be measured against the standards of one's own time. Their greatness was established against the obstacles and defenses of their time, and it would be foolish to try to compare players of one era against performers of another. You can only guess and dream. If you ask any man to pick the greatest players he has ever seen, they will likely be chosen from among his contemporaries—something about reflected glory and all that. For instance, if you ask me who is the greatest lineman I ever saw, I will tell you Bob Suffridge, a guard at Tennessee. We were classmates, and I was an usher at his wedding.*
>
> *"The heaviest of the Four Horsemen weighed about 170 pounds, sometimes said to be nearer to 165. I know they were great, they contributed so much to the game of football, and no one admires the memory of that quartet more than I. As this is written, only Crowley survives. But I would have to tell you that I doubt any of the four could get a scholarship at any major school today. And what does that mean? It means nothing except that those muskets they used at Gettysburg wouldn't help a lot in a battle involving atomic weapons. The march of time really is relentless.* **❞**
>
> *— Hello, Everybody, I'm Lindsey Nelson*
> *© 1985 by Lindsey Nelson*

and embellished them: *'Manning, the 6'-3" Drew red-head, brings 'em to the line . . .'"* He's impressed more than one visiting media member with his recollections of his dad's days at Ole Miss drawn from these tapes.

The announcer who called all of Archie's games at Ole Miss is named Stan Torgerson of Meridian, Mississippi. "It's a kick that this young guy who turned out the way he did got part of his batteries charged by listening to my broadcasts of Archie's games," he said. "Peyton is a great player and a great kid. I'm very impressed with him. I never worried about his talent, more about the possibility of an injury. When I interviewed him, Peyton couldn't have been nicer."

I repeat. When you think about it, there's really a different feeling about the college game, a feeling that's hard to put into words, but it's there nonetheless. You can't manufacture it and nobody really knows how to define it, but you know it when you see it. And, perhaps more importantly, *you know it when you feel it.* It might also be that way in Green Bay, or maybe in Denver, but the pro game is just different. There's something unique about college football.

That's what Lindsey Nelson so perceptively discussed when he penned the words above. The fans bring a unique perspective, a unique frame of reference, to the game, simply because they might have watched many of the players on their favorite team mature before their eyes, some from the time they were born. They were there when many of the great moments in their school's athletic program happened. Traditions are passed down through the generations, so that today's fans can actually speak of the great moments as if they had been there, much the way many of us speak so cogently about events that happened long before our birth.

As Lindsey notes, it may be "reflected glory," but it may also be the times of their lives reflected and played out on the gridiron. I remember having a feeling of pride, if that is the proper word, when many of the 1967 Vol sophomores played a key role in Tennessee winning the SEC title that season. After all, these were the players of my generation, who might have been part of a backyard game or in a high school class mere years earlier, now doing their thing in an

A *post-game moment of reflection after a game at South Carolina.*

on something known as a "chat room" on the Internet, whatever that is. There were, as UT grass guru Bob Campbell once observed, the families who visited the stadium back in 1994 literally to see the grass grow when the real stuff was making its comeback on Shields–Watkins Field. It's no different at Alabama, Auburn, Notre Dame, Michigan, UCLA, USC, or anyplace else.

(Speaking of which, there is, for example, an adopted Vol fan named Mark Ostermeyer in Akron, Iowa, located on the Iowa–Nebraska border, who drove all night to see the 1993 LSU game and went back home right after the game. Before that, he had made the trip just to see the stadium he had seen only on television. He wasn't coming to a game, just wanted to see the stadium. He had become a Vol fan after seeing the 1990 Florida game on the tube. There was also a man named Neal A. Stehling, Jr., who flew in from Guangzhou (Canton), China, for the SEC Championship Game in Atlanta on December 6, 1997. He arrived at 5:30 the morning of the game and returned home the next morning,

Orange jersey on gridirons across the country. My friend Jim Gentry says they are "one of us" and he's right. Every recruiting class is "one of us" to somebody. They become "one of us" as the years pass by.

Earlier, I mentioned players I thought were synonymous with certain jersey numbers. They were, save Peyton, from my college days back in the 1967–70 time frame. They are my frame of reference. That's why it was such fun to talk UT sports with the late Col. Tom Elam or, even today, to do likewise with Bronson Potter. There's something to be said for those who saw both Gene McEver, UT's first All-America and College Football Hall of Fame honoree, and Peyton Manning carry the banner for the Big Orange.

As at most schools, there's the endless debate carried on wherever Vol fans gather, on church steps on Sunday morning, at barber shops across the state of Tennessee, on the local sports talk shows, or even

The *thrill of a Citrus Bowl victory against Ohio State, despite some inclement weather.*

The vintage Peyton Manning passing form.

leaving at 7. Neal booked his flight earlier in the year, certain the Vols would be there. Just for the record, he also booked his flight from Guangzhou to Miami for the Orange Bowl at the same time. Talk about optimism and loyalty.)

It's all a sense of *déjà vu'*, that fancy term for the feeling you get when you think you've been there before. It's great players, great coaches, and great plays. It's the inevitable comparisons. It's the thrill of being part of the game, whether you're sitting on the 50-yard line in Section T or Section U at Neyland Stadium, or on the first row of Section M, right next to where the visiting players come out. (Remember, too, there's never been a goal-line stand on the 50-yard line.)

When the Vols, or whoever your favorite team is, make a great goal-line stand, there's immediate reference to great stands in the past. The same is true with players.

Was Bob Johnson, whom I identified earlier as perhaps the Peyton Manning of his day, the greatest center of all time? Do the linemen of today compare with Eric Still, Antone Davis, Chip Kell, Ed Molinski, or Ted Daffer? Or were Bob Suffridge or Doug Atkins the greatest linemen ever to wear an Orange shirt?

When Al Wilson or Leonard Little knocked a running back backwards, perhaps into another area code, was the hit reminiscent of Steve or Keith De-Long, Steve Kiner, Jack Reynolds, or Andy Spiva?

Who can say? That's the beauty of it all. The comparisons are endless, but that's all part of tradition. Great moments and great plays live on in the mind's eye, ready to be recalled at a moment's notice. There are monikers like "Hack, Mack, and Dodd," Johnny "Blood" Butler, Hank Lauricella, the "New Orleans Flame," John "Drum" Majors, Reggie White, the "Minister of Defense," and many, many more.

▲ *A handshake at midfield after a tough game.*

Which brings us, friends, to Peyton Manning. There's no nickname yet, and, with his influence on the Vol program, he really doesn't need one.

Peyton's career at the University of Tennessee presents a serious challenge to the memory banks, as I try to put everything he did while he was here into proper perspective. There are vignettes, significant happenings, that truly reflect what Peyton meant to everyone he met during his time on campus. His first completion

▲ *A Peyton Manning autographed football for a lucky fan.*

(to James Stewart in the third quarter of the 1994 Florida game), his first TD pass (76 yards to Kendrick Jones in the 1994 Mississippi State game), his first rushing touchdown (a 10-yard run against Kentucky in 1994), his last rushing touchdown (against Vanderbilt on the famous "naked reverse" at the north end in 1997), his last completion (against Nebraska in the 1998 FedEx Orange Bowl to Jamal Lewis, albeit for a loss of four yards), his last TD pass (a five-yarder to Peerless Price earlier in that same game), and all points in between, are all part and parcel of the memories.

There was the electrifying beginning of the 1995 Alabama game (*"80 yards . . . Joey Kent . . . Touchdown . . . on play Number One . . ."* was the way the Vol Network's John Ward called it). There was Peyton directing the band after big wins, two times after wins over Alabama, both in Birmingham, and one after clinching the SEC Championship against Vanderbilt in Neyland

Stadium in 1997. "There was a guy in the back who was off key," he deadpanned. "That was my fault."

There were the "Vol Walks" to Neyland Stadium down what is now Peyton Manning Pass via Volunteer Boulevard and the excitement of trips to the airport and bus rides to and from the stadiums on the road. There was always a gaggle of fans in the lobby of hotels in Columbia, South Carolina, and Springdale, Arkansas. And all venues in between. Vol fans have been there in force, wherever "there" is.

Where do you begin to sort all this out? I began with Bob Johnson, a Vol All-America center in 1966–67, who was, until Peyton, perhaps the most decorated Vol ever. Johnson was a two-time All-America selection, an Academic All-America, two-time Academic All-SEC, an NCAA Post-graduate (1968) and Silver Anniversary Award winner (1993), and a member of the College Football Hall of Fame (1989). He was the

Columbus Touchdown Club's Lineman of the Year way back in 1967.

When Peyton was unable to be present at the Columbus Touchdown Club's 1998 award ceremonies to receive the Club's National Quarterback of the Year Award, Johnson, now president of Imperial Adhesives in Cincinnati and Nashville, attended the awards presentation in Peyton's stead, driving over from Cincinnati.

For perspective's sake, Peyton won the Columbus Touchdown Club's National High School Offensive Player of the Year award in 1993, while Archie won the organization's Collegiate Player of the Year in 1969 and 1970. So there's a Tennessee and a Manning connection to this Award.

"It's a credit to Archie and Olivia, and to Peyton as well, that he's so untainted by everything that's come his way," Johnson said. "He is such a great young man athletically and academically and it's obvious he's been rooted in such terrific values. I was proud to represent him in Columbus and am proud he was at Tennessee. He's a remarkable young man."

I got another perspective from another former Vol, Andy Kozar, who was a pile-driving fullback for the Vols in the final Neyland years (1950–52). After making his mark as a Vol footballer, he was drafted by the Chicago Bears, went into the service in 1953, gained a masters (1955) and Ph.D. (1961) from the University of Michigan, taught there and then returned to Knoxville in 1966 as Dr. Andy Kozar, teaching in the Physical Education Department and working for a while in the president's office. He is now back where he belongs, with a research appointment in Exercise Science.

"This past semester," Dr. Kozar said, "Peyton came to me for an independent studies class in Exercise Science. He wanted to do a project of a historical nature.

▲ *At Ole Miss the day Archie's jersey was retired, September 27, 1986. With Archie (center) that day are (L–R) Ole Miss Chancellor Gerald Turner, Archie's collegiate coach Johnny Vaught, Ole Miss Athletic Director Warner Alford, Olivia, Sis Manning, Archie's mother, Cooper and Peyton.*

Working out with the Colts.

▲ *More preparations for the upcoming season with the Colts.*

Father and son leave the field. ▶

▲ *Three young Mannings watch as their father's jersey is retired.*

He had already shown me that he had a tremendous interest in Tennessee football history. He was really serious about learning as much as he could.

"I had a copy of *Illustrated Football* I was going to show a colleague and Peyton took one look at one of the photographs and said, 'That's Beattie Feathers.' And it was. That shocked me. Peyton told me all about who Beattie Feathers was. Most athletes these days know very little about Tennessee tradition."

But there was more, Dr. Kozar said. "I assigned him the task of interviewing former Vols Doug Atkins and George Cafego. This was last winter just before George died. We went to George's house and he was as excited to see Peyton as Peyton was to see him. He obviously recognized Peyton and his contributions to the University. The interviews reflected that Peyton had read everything he could about both Doug Atkins and George Cafego."

There was one interesting tidbit that Peyton elicited from Cafego (Kozar actually said he "pulled it out of him"). This was the derivation of Cafego's moniker "Bad News." Many people thought he got it for how fast he traveled with a football under his arm. Not so, say the Manning–Cafego interview transcripts.

"Neyland always played one team in the first quarter and another in the second quarter," Kozar said. "In the second quarter of the Kentucky game in Lexington in 1937, Cafego left the game and came back in the second quarter. He was the only player to do so. The public address announcer, noting Cafego's return

▲ *Can this guy throw or what?*

He recalled that Peyton was the star of the show merely by his presence. "All those famous people were there and lined up to get Peyton's autograph, college football players and adults, some great football players in the bunch, alike," Kozar said. "It was one of the most amazing things I've ever seen." All of them, it should be noted, worked to get their picture taken with Peyton.

That night, here's what Peyton in part said when he received the Vincent dePaul Draddy Award in front of a packed house in the Grand Ballroom at the oh-so-posh Waldorf-Astoria Hotel:

"I am truly honored to be chosen the Draddy Scholarship Award recipient. I understand that Mr. Draddy was a former quarterback in 1929 at Manhattan College. I was talking with Brian Griese [Bob Griese's son and a fellow quarterback at Michigan and Division IA Scholar–Athlete nominee] earlier and he and I decided that in 1929 Mr. Draddy probably faced similar academic standards, but probably didn't have to face as many zone blitzes.

"I attended this banquet when I was 12 years old, when my father was inducted into the College Hall of Fame. As he responded that night for the Hall of Fame class, I remembered something he said. 'Football is America's game; football is not about glory, it's about dreams.' Well, college football is about dreams. It's about working hard in the classroom and on the field to make those dreams come true. One of my dreams was to play college football and to be selected a scholar–athlete tonight. I'm truly honored to win the Draddy Award and to stand here tonight to thank all of you for supporting the greatest institution of college football."

Kozar added that Peyton was the "total package. He just epitomizes the All-American boy, the type ath-

to the game, said 'Here comes Bad News.'" That's the story, directly from Cafego himself, via Peyton.

Kozar also recounted what happened at a luncheon for national scholar–athletes he and I attended the day of the National Football Foundation and Hall of Fame Awards Banquet in New York City in December 1997.

In the huddle at the 1997 Citrus Bowl.

▲ *Smokey, long-time Vol mascot, on the sidelines.*

lete that comes along perhaps once in a generation. You just have to like him. I remember reading about Frank Merriwell. Peyton's that kind of guy. He's as near to what you would want your son to be as you could get.

"He stayed the extra year for the right reasons. He won the Sullivan Award as the nation's top amateur athlete and, if you check, you will find that very few football players have won that award."

Dr. Kozar was right. I checked. Other than Peyton, only Charley Ward, the 1993 Heisman winner, Arnold Tucker, quarterback at Army (1946), and Felix "Doc" Blanchard ("Mr. Inside" at Army, 1945), have the word

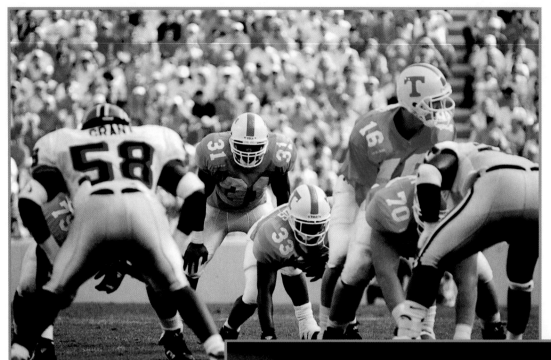

Peyton brings the Vols to the line.

"football" penned in beside their names on the list of winners now totaling 68. Past winners have included speedskaters Dan Jansen (1994) and Bonnie Blair (1992), Ward (1993), Senator and Princeton hoopster Bill Bradley (1965), swimmer Janet Evans (1989), trackster Jackie Joiner-Kersee (1986), decathlete Bruce Jenner (1976), and Olympian and Tennessean Wilma Rudolph (1961). Rudolph joins swimmer Tracy Caulkins (1978) as Sullivan Award winners from Tennessee.

▲ *A video look at Marcus Nash's game-winning reception at the Georgia Dome.*

"The AAU represents 32 sports from the grassroots to the national level," AAU president Bobby Dodd said announcing the 1997 winner. "Peyton exemplifies the best true amateur athlete in all of sport with a commitment to his education and to sportsmanship."

Peyton won the Sullivan Award as the nation's finest amateur athlete as part of a field which included U.S. Swimmer of the Year Chad Carvin of Army, Florida State baseballer J.D. Drew, Wake Forest's hoopster Tim Duncan, World Champion wrestler Les Gutches, Lady Vol basketball player Chamique Holdsclaw, South Carolina softball player Trinity Johnson, disability sports standout Linda Mastandrea, World Champion swimmer Jenny Thompson, and USA Gymnastics all-around national champion Blaine Wilson.

Peyton received the Sullivan Award in Knoxville at a luncheon sponsored by the AAU, the Knoxville Sports

▲ *Peyton looks to the sideline for the play.*

Corporation, and the University of Tennessee on February 25. His remarks, excerpted below, were vintage Peyton, not what you generally get at one of these award ceremonies. It went well beyond what you would expect:

"It's really very humbling when a person is selected to receive an award for something he loves to do. It's even more rewarding for me to receive the Sullivan Award today, because its voters traditionally look beyond statistics and highlights; instead they look at the person and what he or she represents.

"As everybody knows, I passed up going to the pros and supposedly a lot of money in order to stay amateur, to be a

kid one more year and to build more irreplaceable memories. A year ago, it was more important for me to take advantage of my last chance to play college football for no other reason than my love of the game. Not for the money, not because I had to fulfill a commitment—just because I love the game! That's what amateur sports is all about.

"If you know me at all, you probably won't be surprised to hear that I've done a little research on James E. Sullivan, the man this award is named for. He was a pioneer in city playground development and recreational facilities for kids. It seems to me that Mr. Sullivan knew what playing sports is really all about. It's not about being the best. It's about discovering what your best is. It's about dreaming big and doing whatever is necessary day after day to make those dreams come true, whether you have state-of-the-art equipment or just a patch of grass to practice on.

"They say I'm just the fourth football player to have ever received this tremendous award. I hope I won't be the last. There are so many awards given for individual accomplishments. But where are the Halls of Fame for teams? Without my team, I couldn't have accomplished a fraction of what people give me credit for. I'd like to thank all my teammates, coaches, and the entire Tennessee family.

"I know it will be near impossible for many people here at Tennessee to remember me as anything more than a football player. But, in truth, I don't want to be remembered as a quarterback or No. 16. I hope that someday, I'll be remembered as a good person, who happened to play football.

"Don't get me wrong. I'm passionate about football. It's just not my whole life. Too many athletes think that achieving athletic goals is the ultimate accomplishment in life. I believe people can love their sport without making it their life's focus. Athletes can take the many important lessons we learn in sports and apply them to the rest of our lives. Doing that can help make us better people and leaders, and can generate even greater fulfillment and satisfaction.

"An estimated 2.5 million people were on hand in Neyland Stadium during the past four years to watch the Tennessee Volunteers play football. Millions more on TV! So if our actions on the field, and having my name on the Sullivan Trophy inspires others to dream more, do more, and become more, as so many have said, I only hope they don't limit that potential to sports."

When Peyton won the Westwood One Horizon Award back in 1996, given as a "vehicle for recogniz-

▲ *Peyton discusses the flow of the game with linebacker Al Wilson.*

▲ *More than likely, good things are ready to happen for the Vols against Northwestern.*

ing a young man or woman with a bright future in his or her respective sport," here's what the award's sponsors had to say about Peyton, presaging what was to come: "There are quite a few top-rated high school athletes who earn high praise in college football . . . eventually. Usually it takes some time and hard work, but by his junior or senior year, a player can rack up several honors after a lot of time on the playing field. And yet, only a year away from his freshman debut as quarterback for the University of Tennessee, Peyton is already highly acclaimed, already a candidate for the Heisman Trophy."

The statement goes on to say that Manning is out to do more than " . . . follow in his father's footsteps.

It's no wonder that expectations are high when Manning steps out on the turf at Neyland Stadium and performs for the third largest college football crowds in the country."

There's more. "In just two years, Manning has proven that he has more than athletic prowess. In 1995, he added to what is rapidly becoming a long list of accomplishments by making the SEC Academic Honor Roll with a 3.49 in Business Management. He also takes the UT Volunteer name seriously, spending some time visiting the Morgan County Regional Correction Facility."

On the University of Tennessee flagship campus in Knoxville, the Torchbearer statue, complete with eter-

▲ *Jamal Lewis gets ready to hit the hole.*

have displayed unfaltering and effective devotion to the best interest of both the institution and the student body. Moreover, they are possessed of faithfulness, initiative, courage, energy, integrity, and modesty in an unusual degree—as disclosed by their activity in general student and University affairs and the confidence imposed in them by faculty and students. The selection has been made after much careful, discriminating investigation and balancing of characteristics and contributions. It is felt that these seniors are truly reflective of the motto: 'He who beareth a torch shadoweth himself to give light to others.'"

Each potential recipient is asked to "describe **ONE ACTIVITY** in which she/he has participated that best exemplifies the spirit of the Torchbearer Award." Here's what Peyton Manning wrote to the Committee as part of his nomination:

"As a student–athlete at Tennessee, I have truly enjoyed the numerous opportu-

nal flame, has stood since 1968 on Volunteer Boulevard in Circle Park at the top of what is now Peyton Manning Pass. The classes of 1928 through 1932 had given $1,000 to be used as a prize for a sculpture that would "capture the spirit of University youth and its ideal of service."

Each year since 1931, the University of Tennessee honors its top graduates with the designation "Torchbearer," according to the following criteria:

"TORCHBEARERS are seniors who in an outstanding fashion represent their Alma Mater. They are students who

▲ *Vol defenders close ranks for the tackle.*

▲ *Manning and Leonard Little meet the press after the SEC Championship Game.*

nities for community involvement that I have received. I have enjoyed giving back to the University and the community what they have given me through constant support and dedication. It is difficult for me to pinpoint one specific activity that best exemplifies my giving spirit. However, I do feel that my community service, whether it be speaking to youth about drugs, teaching high school students the importance of study skills, giving my testimony to churches, or visiting ill patients at hospitals, portrays the spirit of a Torchbearer.

"Through my continuous involvement in the community, I have been able to be a great Ambassador for the University of Tennessee. I have attempted to portray the positive aspects of the football program as well as the entire University in all my endeavors.

"My main mission in speaking at area schools has been to help the students understand that I am not just a football

player, but that I am a student and a common person. Successful accomplishment of this goal allows me to set an example for students to follow, whether it be abstaining from drug use, remaining serious about my education, or simply becoming involved in the community.

"My speeches at local schools are based on priorities. I feel that setting priorities helps me to keep every aspect of my life on track. I have preached the importance of prioritizing faith, family, education, and social life priorities, in this order. Hopefully, the students understand that football is only a fraction of my life and I rank it along with my social responsibilities. I stress the importance of faith, family, and education. I feel that I have successfully impacted at least a few students, hopefully more, but if I can help change even one student from drugs, violence, or other problems, I consider what I've done a success.

Manning explains how the game unfolded.

A real life view of Marcus Nash motoring toward the game-winning TD against Auburn.

"One of the most difficult tasks I have faced while helping the community has been visiting seriously ill patients in the hospital. Hopefully, I have given these patients some feeling of happiness through my visits. I have seen several children with different types of cancer, I have visited birthday parties for terminally ill children, and I visited a young boy who was paralyzed on a hiking trip. Each of these visits was extremely difficult because I was exposed to the pain and suffering that these patients and families have experienced, but I am excited to bring hope into their lives.

"I hope that I have been able to portray my giving spirit through this short essay. I feel that my extensive involvement in the activities of the University of Tennessee, as well as the surrounding community, definitely exemplifies the Spirit of the Torchbearer Award."

I thought about that essay when I read what *Sports Illustrated* had to say about Texas runningback Ricky Williams in a May issue, in a college football story written by Tim Layden.

"To idealistic fans, Williams is the latest in a short line of stars (Peyton Manning and Tim Duncan), who exemplify what's good about college sports by foregoing the pro draft and instant wealth, and staying in school," is what Layden wrote about Williams. It is similar to many of the stories written about Manning.

Consider me one of the "idealists." The Peyton Manning story is proof positive that the good guys can

▲ *The Beer Barrel is the spoils of the Tennessee–Kentucky game each year.*

have a beneficial impact on a college campus and the state as a whole.

When the history of the Class of 1997 was written, Peyton Manning's three-year undergraduate tenure, his department-leading GPA (3.61 in Speech Communication), Phi Beta Kappa status, and enviable record of campus and community service earned him a Chancellor's Citation for "Extraordinary Campus Leadership and Service." His time on the Hill also earned him the respect and admiration of everybody with whom he came into contact. You really can't ask for anything more. That's about all you can say. Jay Burns and future recipients of the Peyton Manning Scholarship will be the living testimonies to Peyton's impact and influence.

Time passed quickly from April 18, the day of the NFL draft and the night of his recognition at the spring game. Media reports noted his participation in a Colts' mini-camp and lamented the fact he could not report until June 1, the graduation deadline for his original class, the Class of 1998.

Media reports also noted that Vol fans were making serious inquiries about Indianapolis Colts season tickets (after all, Knoxville is not really that far from Indiana's largest city), and it was also noted that a local radio station would have the radio broadcasts and a local television stadium would broadcast the Colts' games each Sunday. Talk about your positive impact.

When all is said and done, what do we make of Peyton? He came back. He came back, as Dr. Kozar noted, for the right reasons. He was a team player. He never was bigger than the team and the program. He understood what college football was all about.

▲ *Marcus Nash grabs this Manning toss for the first score against Georgia in 1997.*

"I thought I didn't have enough memories," Peyton said last December. "That's why I wanted to come back, to create some more memories."

He was never really about individual awards, that wasn't his motivation. He said as much more than once.

"This isn't about going out and trying to win individual awards," he said before the 1997 season. "You do that, you start making bad decisions. On third-and-10, instead of throwing the ball away, you force one down the middle. You're trying to be a hero and you get picked off. I'm not into that. I've always been a team guy. And this is about being disappointed in our two losses last year. I am wrapped up in that."

There is a bond between brothers that is hard to pinpoint, but it's always there. Peyton's also

wrapped up in that. The Manning brothers are no exception.

There was a time in the mid-1990s that the family came to a crossroads. The focal point was Peyton's older brother Cooper. In his SI article, Layden sets the scene. Peyton, then a sophomore, had thrown an interception and Newman had lost a playoff game. It was a crusher.

Cooper, then a senior, put his arm around Peyton and told him everything was fine. Cooper went on to Ole Miss, practiced with the team, and dressed for a game. There was a problem: spinal stenosis, a congenital narrowing of the spinal cavity. His career was over just like that.

Before he left to go back to Ole Miss, Cooper wrote the following note and left it for Peyton. Here it is, as only a brother could pen it:

"I would like to live my dream of playing football through you. Although I cannot play anymore, I know I can still get the same feeling out of watching my little brother do what he does best. I know now that we are good for each other, because I need you to be serious and look at things from a different perspective. I am good for you, as well, to take things light. I love you, Peyt, and only great things lie ahead for you. Thanks for everything on and off the field."

Vol fans can express similar sentiment to Peyton. They have thrilled to his accomplishments on and off the field and his welcome at the season finale against Vanderbilt and the 1998 Orange and White game was one way of saying "Thanks for the memories." Vol fans remember their heroes fondly, even if it's just turning to their compatriots and saying "That Manning boy can really play the game." It's true—that Manning boy can really play the game!

They will remember the young man from New Orleans who led the Vols to victory in game after game, three New Year's Day bowl games in as many years and one who always made Vol fans proud.

"Peyton has a freshness about him," UT Sports Information Director Bud Ford, who oversaw Peyton's media relations on the Hill, said. "He handles the attention as well as anyone I've ever been around. He's prompt and courteous. And if someone asks him for the millionth time what it's like to be Archie Manning's son, he won't roll his eyes and get impatient. He'll just smile and answer the question."

Even before lining up against Peyton, Nebraska's Grant Wistrom, a man who goes after quarterbacks with a certain sound and fury, said of his Orange Bowl opponent: "There are just certain guys that when they're on the field, they pick up the whole level of the football team. He's one of those type people ... He's a difference-maker out there.

"He's had more pressure than probably anybody in the history of college football placed upon him, and I think he's done extremely well with it. He's just as famous as any NFL quarterback. That kind of pressure and scrutiny placed upon a person would be kind of tough, but he handled it extremely well. In my mind, he's one of the best players in college football this year, if not the best."

Difference-maker. Leader. Loyal. Family-oriented. Focused. Prepared. Those are just some of the adjectives that leap out at you when you talk about Peyton Manning. I know, because I've seen all of them manifested in him during his career. His time here has been a vintage time in Tennessee football, something no one could have expected to have happened the way it did.

As Lindsey says, the march of time is really relentless. Let's see now. I've seen both Archie and Peyton Manning do their thing in Neyland Stadium

▲ *Jamal Lewis does his thing against Georgia.*

in a 30-year period. That's not quite Gene McEver and Peyton, but it will do.

It all began in the Rose Bowl in Pasadena, California, and ended in the Orange Bowl in Miami, Florida. It continued through Sanford Stadium in Athens, Georgia, Scott Field in Starkville, Mississippi, Williams–Brice Stadium in Columbia, South Carolina, Vanderbilt Stadium in Nashville, Florida Field (one of only two venues where the Vols have been both home team and visitor), Razorback Stadium in Fayetteville,

Arkansas, Legion Field in Birmingham, Alabama, Commonwealth Stadium in Lexington, Kentucky, the Citrus Bowl in Orlando, Florida, Liberty Bowl Memorial Stadium in Memphis, War Memorial Stadium in Little Rock, and, of course, Neyland Stadium in Knoxville. Fourteen venues in all. If you saw him play at any or all of these venues, consider yourself lucky. There were 2,508,414 who saw his 25 games at Neyland Stadium. Another 1,252,071 saw him play on the road. Another 343,765 saw him play in bowl games or in the SEC Championship Game. That's 4,104,250 in all.

There was a lot of excitement in those games, a lot of memories. After all, wasn't that what Peyton was looking for, to create memories? If that were the case, he certainly succeeded, for himself and for Vol fans. If that were the mission, mission accomplished. He's made a difference, made things better for all of us. For my part, I say "Thanks, Peyton." As the scripture says, you have fought the fight, kept the faith, and finished the course. Well done.

T.J.M.
Knoxville, Tennessee
May 1998

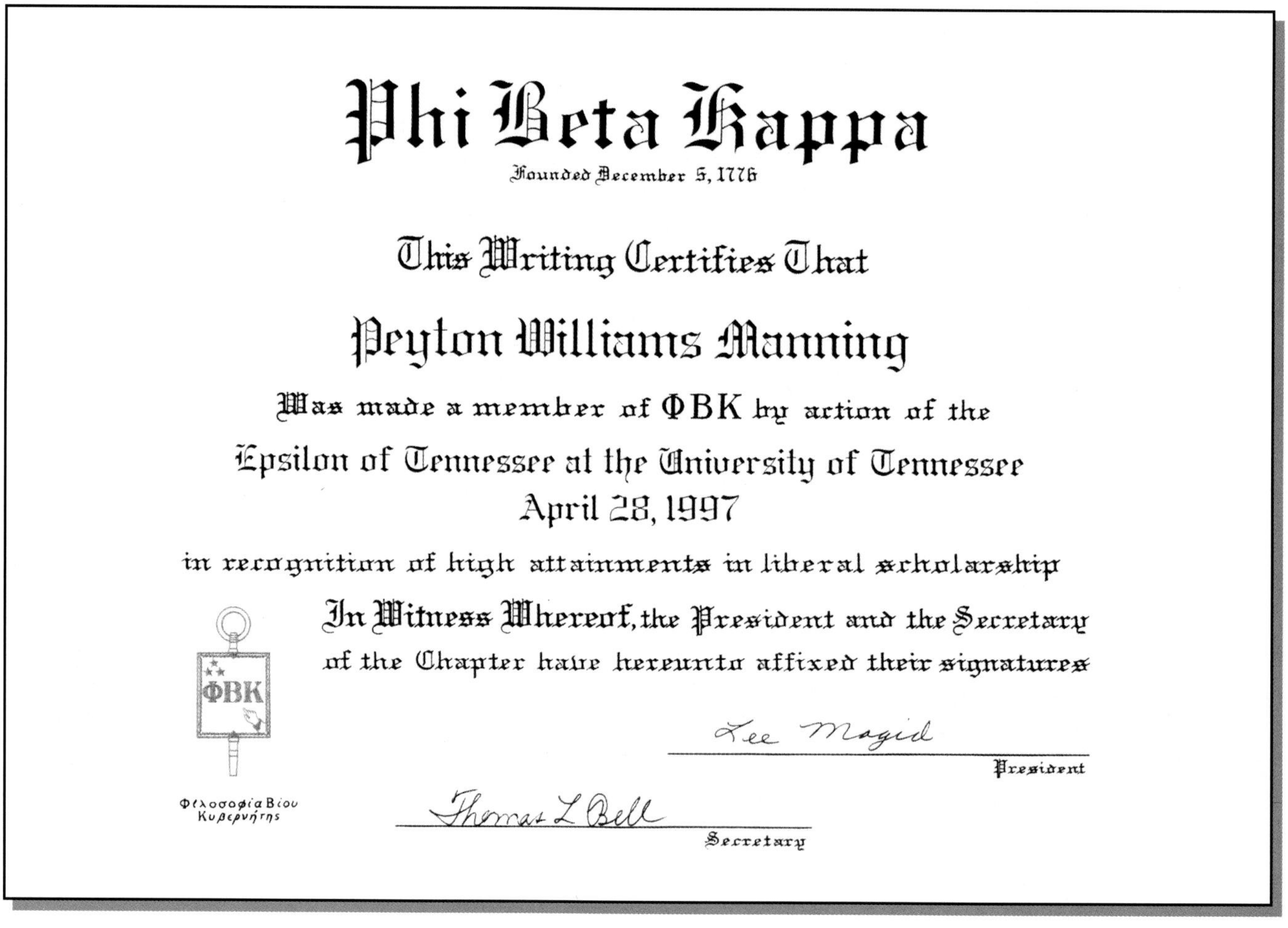

Phi Beta Kappa

Founded December 5, 1776

This Writing Certifies That

Peyton Williams Manning

Was made a member of ΦBK by action of the

Epsilon of Tennessee at the University of Tennessee
April 28, 1997

in recognition of high attainments in liberal scholarship

In Witness Whereof, the President and the Secretary of the Chapter have hereunto affixed their signatures

Lee Magid
President

Thomas L Bell
Secretary

Φιλοσοφία Βίου
Κυβερνήτης

The panoply of Neyland Stadium is reflected in the band's tuba section.

PEYTON'S TOP 10 GAMES

LISTED IN CHRONOLOGICAL ORDER

▲ *What the opposition doesn't want: Peyton with the ball in his hand looking for a receiver.*

The Facts: Tennessee made things happen on both sides of the ball to take an impressive victory over Arkansas that raised the Vol ledger to 3 and 3. The Vols turned things around with a 21-point second quarter that saw Peyton Manning throw a TD pass to Mose Phillips and send Phillips and James Stewart into the end zone on short runs. Tyrone Hines scored on a fumble recovery and Stewart caught a 27-yard TD pass from Manning. Peyton completed 12 of 19 passes for 157 yards and John Becksvoort added a field goal. Vol defenders forced six Arkansas turnovers sparked by capable performances from Ben Talley, Scott Galyon, George Kidd, and Jason Parker. The Vols also converted six of 13 third-down opportunities.

THE NUMBERS:

ARKANSAS	0	7	0	14	*21*
TENNESSEE	7	21	10	0	*38*

UT—Phillips, run 5. Becksvoort kick. UT—Phillips, pass from Manning 23. Becksvoort kick. UT—Hines, fumble return 38. Becksvoort kick. ARK—Malone, run 24. Ellison kick. UT—J. Stewart, run 1. Becksvoort kick. UT—J. Stewart, pass from Manning 27. Becksvoort kick. UT—Becksvoort, FG 34. ARK—C. Johnson, pass from Reed 82. Ellison kick. ARK—Reed, run 18. Ellison kick.

GAME STATISTICS

UT		ARK
24	First Downs	18
50–221	Rushing (Attempts–Net Yards)	47–230
28–16–2	Passing (Attempts–Completions–Interceptions)	19–11–0
211	Passing Yards	200
78	Total Offensive Plays	66
432	Total Offensive Yards	430
4–39.0	Punts—Average	4–45.6
4–40	Penalties—Yards	2–10
3–3	Fumbles—Lost	7–6
6–13	Third-Down Conversions	3–11

SIGNIFICANCE: *This was Manning's first SEC victory and continued a streak that saw the Vols recovering from an early 1 and 3 record.*

TENNESSEE 45, VIRGINIA TECH 23
FLORIDA FIELD/THE GATOR BOWL
GAINESVILLE, FLORIDA
DECEMBER 30, 1994
ATTENDANCE: 62,200

The Facts: After a 1 and 3 start, the Vols had won six of their final seven games to secure the bid to play the Hokies, knocking off Kentucky and Vanderbilt by 117 to 0 to get there. Once the game started, the Vols dominated the proceedings from start to finish, scoring on five of their first seven possessions. Manning completed 12 of 19 passes for 189 yards and threw a 36-yard TD pass to Marcus Nash. He had a 42-yarder to Joey Kent the play before Nash's TD grab that was perhaps the most spectacular grab of the evening. The Vol defense was paced by Tyrone Hines, who was in on 13 tackles and had an interception to set up the Vols' first TD. The Vols scored points in bunches in the first half, putting 35 points on the board in possession time of 11:46.

THE NUMBERS:

VIRGINIA TECH	0	10	6	7	*23*
TENNESSEE	14	21	0	10	*45*

UT—J. Stewart, run 1. Becksvoort kick. UT—Nash, pass from Manning 36. Becksvoort kick. UT—Graham, run 1. Becksvoort kick. VT—Thomas, run 1. Williams kick. UT—J. Stewart, run 1. Becksvoort kick. UT—Jones, pass from J. Stewart 19. Becksvoort kick. VT—Williams, FG 28. VT—DeShazo, run 7. Kick failed. UT—J. Stewart, run 5. Becksvoort kick. UT—Becksvoort, FG 19. VT—Still, pass from Druckenmiller 9. Williams kick.

GAME STATISTICS

UT		VT
18	First Downs	22
47–245	Rushing (Attempts–Net Yards)	43–189
23–16–0	Passing (Attempts–Completions–Interceptions)	38–23–2
250	Passing Yards	237
70	Total Offensive Plays	81
495	Total Offensive Yards	426
5–43.6	Punts—Average	5–43.4
7–58	Penalties—Yards	3–25
0–0	Fumbles—Lost	5–1
7–14	Third-Down Conversions	6–16

SIGNIFICANCE: *Played at Florida Field because of renovations to the Gator Bowl in Jacksonville, the game marked continued improvement by Manning, who had been thrust into the limelight early in his UT career. He was named SEC "Freshman of the Year," and his performance under center that night gave insight into what was to come for the Vols over the next three years.*

The Facts: In the Vols' first-ever visit to Fayetteville, Peyton Manning twice led the Vols back from 10-point deficits, with the white-shirted Orangemen outscoring the Razorbacks 35 to 7 to finally take the 18-point win. Manning ran a steady offense that rang up 521 yards overall. He completed 35 of 46 passes for 384 yards for his day's work, including two TD passes to Kent and single tosses to Eric Lane and Maurice Staley. Jay Graham scored the game's final three TDs on short runs as the Vol offensive line dominated in the trenches. They trailed 24 to 14 with 6:07 left in the second quarter before rallying for the win. Jay Graham ran for 130 yards and three scores and Kent caught a school-record-tying 13 passes for 161 yards and two scores.

THE NUMBERS:

TENNESSEE	7	21	7	14	*49*
ARKANSAS	14	10	0	7	*31*

UT—Kent, pass from Manning 55. Hall kick. UA—Hill, pass from Lunney 26. Latourette kick. UA—Lucas, pass from Lunney 52. Latourette kick. UA—Latourette, FG 36. UT—Kent, pass from Manning 29. Hall kick. UA—Lucas, pass from Lunney 30. Latourette kick. UT—Lane, pass from Manning 7. Hall kick. UT—Staley, pass from Manning 11. Hall kick. UT—Graham, run 1. Hall kick. UT—Graham, run 2. Hall kick. UA—Hill, run 3. Latourette kick. UT—Graham, run 5. Hall kick.

GAME STATISTICS

UT		UA
32	First Downs	19
40–137	Rushing (Attempts–Net Yards)	32–50
46–35–1	Passing (Attempts–Completions–Interceptions)	32–24–0
384	Passing Yards	290
86	Total Offensive Plays	64
521	Total Offensive Yards	340
4–35.8	Punts—Average	5–39.4
8–88	Penalties—Yards	8–52
3–0	Fumbles—Lost	3–1
10–15	Third-Down Conversions	4–13

SIGNIFICANCE: *Manning had an answer for everything the Razorback defenders threw at him en route to the 18-point win and comebacks from 10 points down twice in the first half. With Alabama coming the next week, this game had loomed as definite upset material.*

TENNESSEE 41, ALABAMA 14
LEGION FIELD
BIRMINGHAM, ALABAMA
OCTOBER 14, 1995
ATTENDANCE: 83,091

The Facts: Tennessee hit the Tide with a haymaker on the first play and moved from there to the one-sided victory. Manning found Kent for an 80-yard TD on play number one and when the Tide closed to 28 to 14 late in the third quarter Jay Graham raced 75 yards for the game-clinching score. Manning had two TD tosses to Marcus Nash and scored on a naked bootleg at left end in the first quarter. It was a game in which Manning literally did everything, including directing the band after the game in an impromptu celebration at the northeast corner of Legion Field. For the night, Manning completed 20 of 29 passes for 301 yards and Graham rushed for 114. Manning's TD run came after a brilliant fake to Graham after which Peyton scooted to his left for the score, leaving everybody, including the officials, wondering where the ball was.

THE NUMBERS:

TENNESSEE	21	7	7	6	*41*
ALABAMA	0	7	7	0	*14*

UT—Kent, pass from Manning 80. Hall kick. UT—Nash, pass from Manning 25. Hall kick. UT—Manning, run 1. Hall kick. UA—Key, pass from Kitchens 2. Proctor kick. UT—Nash, pass from Manning 30. Hall kick. UA—Madden, run 15. Proctor kick. UT—Graham, run 75. Hall kick. UT—Hall, FG 25. UT—Hall, FG 37.

GAME STATISTICS

UT		UA
21	First Downs	21
37–167	Rushing (Attempts–Net Yards)	32–75
30–21–0	Passing (Attempts–Completions–Interceptions)	48–24–3
329	Passing Yards	228
67	Total Offensive Plays	80
496	Total Offensive Yards	303
3–41.3	Punts—Average	3–39.7
6–40	Penalties—Yards	7–31
3–1	Fumbles—Lost	3–2
4–13	Third-Down Conversions	8–17

SIGNIFICANCE: *It was the Vols' first win in Birmingham and likewise in the series since 1985. Not since 1969 had the Vols jumped to a 21 to 0 lead in the first quarter, winning that contest by the strikingly familiar score of 41 to 14.*

TENNESSEE 20, OHIO STATE 14
THE CITRUS BOWL
ORLANDO, FLORIDA
JANUARY 1, 1996
ATTENDANCE: 70,797

The Facts: On a rainy day in Orlando, Jay Graham ran 69 yards for a score, Manning threw a 47-yard TD pass to Kent, Jeff Hall kicked two field goals, and the Vol defenders did the rest as the Vols knocked off the Big 10 co-champs in the first gridiron meeting between the two schools. The Vol defenders forced three Ohio State turnovers in the fourth quarter to seal the issue. The Vols closed the season 11 to 1, the best mark since 1989, and the fifth 11–win season in Tennessee history. The game was played on a Big Orange day in Orange County with a steady rain that got heavy at times. Manning had his TD pass to Kent just after halftime and sent Graham off tackle for his score moments before halftime. The Vols held the high-powered Ohio State offense to 89 yards rushing, 246 yards overall.

THE NUMBERS:

OHIO STATE	7	0	0	7	*14*
TENNESSEE	0	7	7	6	*20*

OSU—George, run 2. Jackson kick. UT—Graham, run 69. Hall kick. UT—Kent, pass from Manning 47. Hall kick. OSU—Dudley, pass from Hoying 32. Jackson kick. UT—Hall, FG 29. UT—Hall, FG 25.

GAME STATISTICS

UT		OSU
15	First Downs	17
32–145	Rushing (Attempts–Net Yards)	36–89
35–20–0	Passing (Attempts–Completions–Interceptions)	38–19–1
182	Passing Yards	246
67	Total Offensive Plays	74
327	Total Offensive Yards	335
9–34.9	Punts—Average	7–48.1
8–43	Penalties—Yards	6–57
1–1	Fumbles—Lost	5–3
5–17	Third-Down Conversions	4–15

SIGNIFICANCE: *Two big plays on offense and a key stop by Bill Duff on Heisman Trophy winner Eddie George proved to be the difference in the first-ever meeting between the two teams. The win vaulted the Vols to second in the CNN-USA Today poll and third in the AP poll.*

TENNESSEE 41, MISSISSIPPI 3
LIBERTY BOWL MEMORIAL STADIUM
MEMPHIS, TENNESSEE
OCTOBER 3, 1996
ATTENDANCE: 62,640

The Facts: Leading 17 to 3 early in the third quarter, the Vols scored 21 points in the third quarter to move ahead 31 to 3 and take the nocturnal contest in Memphis against his father's and mother's alma mater. An interception by Craig King led to the Vols' first score and Peyton Manning found Marcus Nash for a score shortly after intermission. For the night, Peyton was 22 of 28 passing for 282 yards. Bill Duff recovered a fumble for a Vol score and Leonard Little was SEC Defensive Player of the Week for a five-tackle, three-sack, one lost-yard tackle, and two forced-fumbles performance that was one of the dominating performances of the season.

THE NUMBERS:

TENNESSEE	3	14	21	3	*41*
MISSISSIPPI	0	3	0	0	*3*

UT—Hall, FG 24. MISS—Montz, FG 40. UT—Lane, run 31. Hall kick. UT—Graham, run 1. Hall kick. UT—Nash, pass from Manning 5. Hall kick. UT—Duff, fumble return 4. Hall kick. UT—Levine, run 7. Hall kick. UT—Hall, FG 38.

GAME STATISTICS

UT		UM
25	First Downs	11
45–221	Rushing (Attempts–Net Yards)	34–64
28–22–0	Passing (Attempts–Completions–Interceptions)	26–14–1
282	Passing Yards	120
73	Total Offensive Plays	60
503	Total Offensive Yards	184
2–43.0	Punts—Average	7–39.7
13–104	Penalties—Yards	8–66
1–1	Fumbles—Lost	3–3
4–11	Third-Down Conversions	2–14

SIGNIFICANCE: *It was an emotion-filled night for the Manning family, one that saw the Vols break the game open defensively in the second half.*

TENNESSEE 48, NORTHWESTERN 28
THE CITRUS BOWL
ORLANDO, FLORIDA
JANUARY 1, 1997
ATTENDANCE: 63,467

The Facts: Tennessee jumped to a 21 to 0 first quarter lead, saw Northwestern tie the game 21 to 21 in the second quarter, then scored the game's next 20 points to take the victory on a day better suited for football than the Vols and Ohio State had faced a year earlier. Peyton Manning, who completed 27 of 39 passes for 408 yards and four scores, found Peerless Price for 43 yards, Joey Kent for 11 and 67 yards and Dustin Moore for six yards. He completed a vintage day with one of his patented fake handoffs to the near side, followed by a 10-yard run to the far boundary for the score. Manning's passing yardage was the second highest of his career to date and a Vol bowl record. Tyrone Hines had an interception and TD run on the first series of the second half. The Vols finished 10 to 2 and were ninth in both final national polls.

THE NUMBERS:

TENNESSEE	21	10	7	10	*48*
NORTHWESTERN	0	21	0	7	*28*

UT—P. Price, pass from Manning 43. Hall kick. UT—Manning, run 10. Hall kick. UT—Kent, pass from Manning 11. Hall kick. NU—D. Autry, run 2. Gowins kick. NU—B. Musso, pass from Schnur 20. Gowins kick. NU—D. Autry, run 28. Gowins kick. UT—Kent, pass from Manning 67. Hall kick. UT—Hall, FG 19. UT—Hines, interception return 30. Hall kick. UT—Hall, FG 28. NU—Bates, pass from Schnur 22. Gowins kick. UT—Moore, pass from Manning 6. Hall kick.

GAME STATISTICS

UT		NU
29	First Downs	22
32–115	Rushing (Attempts–Net Yards)	28–43
39–27–0	Passing (Attempts–Completions–Interceptions)	51–27–4
408	Passing Yards	242
71	Total Offensive Plays	79
523	Total Offensive Yards	285
4–35.8	Punts—Average	6–37.3
13–112	Penalties—Yards	5–40
4–2	Fumbles—Lost	1–1
5–11	Third-Down Conversions	8–19

SIGNIFICANCE: *The contest marked the second straight bowl game against the Big 10 co-champ and the second victory in as many tries. The Vols had two many, by far, offensive weapons for the Wildcats to handle.*

TENNESSEE 38, GEORGIA 13
NEYLAND STADIUM
KNOXVILLE, TENNESSEE
OCTOBER 11, 1997
ATTENDANCE: 106,656

The Facts: In a solid offensive and defensive showing, the Vols hit the Bulldogs with a near-perfect ground and aerial game to take the 25-point decision. Manning had four TD tosses and Jamal Lewis had 232 yards rushing (most ever by a Vol true freshman) against his homestate team to lead the Vol attack. He had four runs over 30 yards on the day. Manning ran the Vol attack with precision, completing 31 of 40 passes for 343 yards and four TDs, one each to Nash, Cedrick Wilson, Peerless Price and Derrick Edmonds. Manning added a TD on a 1-yard run. The Vols had 628 yards total offense and a school-record 35 first downs.

THE NUMBERS:

GEORGIA	3	7	0	3	*13*
TENNESSEE	7	17	0	14	*38*

UT—Nash, pass from Manning 13. Hall kick. UGA—Hines, FG 29. UT—Hall, FG 42. UGA—Edwards, run 49. Hines kick. UT—C. Wilson, pass from Manning 8. Hall kick. UT—Price, pass from Manning 8. Hall kick. UGA—Hines, FG 28. UT—Manning, run 1. Hall kick. UT—Edmonds, pass from Manning 15. Hall kick.

GAME STATISTICS

UT		UGA
35	First Downs	21
36–285	Rushing (Attempts–Net Yards)	30–153
40–31–1	Passing (Attempts–Completions–Interceptions)	34–21–0
343	Passing Yards	288
76	Total Offensive Plays	64
628	Total Offensive Yards	441
1–50.0	Punts—Average	4–43.0
7–60	Penalties—Yards	7–57
0–0	Fumbles—Lost	0–0
7–9	Third-Down Conversions	5–13

SIGNIFICANCE: *The win saw the Vols exhibit exceptional offensive balance and stretch their winning streak against Georgia to seven. Lewis showed Vol fans that he was the real deal with his performances against Mississippi and Georgia.*

TENNESSEE 59, KENTUCKY 31
COMMONWEALTH STADIUM
LEXINGTON, KENTUCKY
NOVEMBER 22, 1997
ATTENDANCE: 61,076

The Facts: In a classic offensive shootout, Peyton Manning outdueled Kentucky's heralded sophomore Tim Couch as the two teams combined for 1021 yards passing and 1329 yards overall. Manning threw five TD passes, three to Marcus Nash (59, 66, and 31 yards) and one each to Jamal Lewis (50 yards) and Andy McCullough (17 yards). Lewis, for his part, rushed for 128 yards on 21 carries and scored three rushing touchdowns, in addition to his 50-yard TD catch from Peyton. The Vols had the ball just over 25 minutes, but ran 65 plays. Manning completed 25 of 35 passes for 523 yards and the aforementioned five TDs. A 21 to 3 bulge in the third quarter proved to be a big difference for the Vols in getting the momentum of the game on their side.

THE NUMBERS:

TENNESSEE	17	7	21	14	*59*
KENTUCKY	7	14	3	7	*31*

UK—Homer, pass from Couch 37. Hanson kick. UT—Hall, FG 49. UT—Nash, pass from Manning 59. Hall kick. UT—McCullough, pass from Manning 17. Hall kick. UK—Sanford, pass from Couch 87. Hanson kick. UT—Nash, pass from Manning 66. Hall kick. UK—White, run 3. Hanson kick. UT—Lewis, pass from Manning 50. Hall kick. UT—Lewis, run 1. Hall kick. UK—Hanson, FG 39. UT—Nash, pass from Manning 31. Hall kick. UK—White, run 1. Hanson kick. UT—Lewis, run 1. Hall kick. UT—Lewis, run 21. Hall kick.

GAME STATISTICS

UT		UK
30	First Downs	27
29–150	Rushing (Attempts–Net Yards)	33–158
36–26–0	Passing (Attempts–Completions–Interceptions)	50–35–3
545	Passing Yards	476
65	Total Offensive Plays	83
695	Total Offensive Yards	634
2–38.0	Punts—Average	2–55.0
4–45	Penalties—Yards	9–56
2–2	Fumbles—Lost	1–0
5–8	Third-Down Conversions	8–16

SIGNIFICANCE: *The win kept the Vols in first place in the SEC Eastern Division and kept championship hopes alive. There was one ominous note. After this game, Manning lost ground to Michigan's Charles Woodson in the Heisman poll.*

TENNESSEE 30, AUBURN 29
THE GEORGIA DOME
ATLANTA, GEORGIA
DECEMBER 6, 1997
ATTENDANCE: 74,896

The Facts: Tennessee came back twice from 10-point deficits to win the SEC Championship before a record SEC Championship crowd in Atlanta. The game-winner came on Peyton Manning's 73-yard toss to Marcus Nash with 11:41 left in the game, on which Nash slipped a tackle and found the wide open spaces down the far sideline. The Vols survived six turnovers and held the Tigers to minus 15 yards rushing for the evening with just 66 in the second half. The game marked the Vols' third league title in the past 10 years. Manning completed 25 of 43 passes for 373 yards and four TDs, with two to Peerless Price and one to Jeremaine Copeland before the game-winner to Nash.

THE NUMBERS:

TENNESSEE	7	3	13	7	*30*
AUBURN	13	7	9	0	*29*

UT—Price, pass from Manning 40. Hall kick. AU—Holmes, FG 30. AU—Ware, fumble recovery 24. Holmes kick. AU—Holmes, FG 48. AU—Goodson, pass from Craig 51. Holmes kick. UT—Hall, FG 27. UT—Copeland, pass from Manning 5. Hall kick. UA—Beasley, pass from Craig 24. Holmes kick. UT—Price, pass from Manning 46. Kick blocked. AU—Reese, return of blocked PAT. UT—Nash, pass from Manning 73. Hall kick.

GAME STATISTICS

UT		AU
22	First Downs	9
36–129	Rushing (Attempts–Net Yards)	21-(-15)
43–25–2	Passing (Attempts–Completions–Interceptions)	34–14–0
373	Passing Yards	262
79	Total Offensive Plays	55
502	Total Offensive Yards	247
5–36.4	Punts—Average	10–43.8
9–49	Penalties—Yards	12–78
6–4	Fumbles—Lost	5–1
9–17	Third-Down Conversions	1–13

SIGNIFICANCE: *The narrow win brought the SEC title back to Knoxville. It was the second crown for the Vols in the 1990s and 12th overall in school history. It was the Vols' third victory over Auburn in the last four tries, the last coming in 1991. Manning also banged up a knee during the contest, a malady which would afflict him through preparations for the Orange Bowl game against Nebraska.*

AUTOGRAPHS